TOWARDS THE MOON WITH FELLINI

Towards the Moon with Fellini

Adventure into the Cosmic Unknown

A Memoir

CHRISTINA ENGELHARDT

WITH JIM MARTYKA

Beverly Hills, California

B.C. Engelhardt & Publisher
Beverly Hills, CA

Cover design by Calvin York Uy
Printed by C-M Books, Chelsea, Michigan

Library of Congress Control Number: TXul-965-153

ISBN: 978-1-7331875-0-3
eISBN: 978-1-7331875-1-0

First Printing 2019

*My eternal gratitude of friendship
to Federico and to You.*

CONTENTS

Acknowledgments ix

Foreword xi

Introduction xiii

Chapter 1—You Are Now Part of Something Important. 1

Chapter 2—Christ-in-an-Angel-Heart. 9

Chapter 3—You Should Be a Model 17

Chapter 4—My Own Harmonic Convergence 27

Chapter 5—It Begins in the City of Angels 35

Chapter 6—The Pink One Meets the Green One 45

Chapter 7—A Journey Off the Path 53

Chapter 8—I See You 57

Chapter 9—The Trip to Tulum 63

Chapter 10—Che Diavolo Ci Facciamo Qui? 73

Chapter 11—A Symphony of Colors 81

Chapter 12—You Must Go to Him Now 87

Chapter 13—Understanding the Colors 93

Chapter 14—You Are One of Us. 99

Chapter 15—Reconnecting in Rome 107

Chapter 16—What Did I Do? 115

Chapter 17—Midnight at Café Greco and an Act of Defiance 121

Chapter 18—The Power of the Voice 127

Chapter 19—Sharing the Story 133

Chapter 20—Life in Italy, Life in the Papers 149

Chapter 21—Eight, Eight, Eighty-Eight. 153

Chapter 22—An American Artist in Italy 161

Chapter 23—The Colors Fade 165

Chapter 24—La Voce della Luna. 173

Chapter 25—Verso la Luna con Fellini. 179

Chapter 26—Silence and Catharsis. 185

Chapter 27—Join Us, Lead Us, Leave It All Behind 191

Chapter 28—Fellini's Lost and Last Film. 197

Chapter 29—Is You Gone?. 203

Chapter 30—Living in Fear 207

Chapter 31—New and Powerful Friends. 213

Chapter 32—The Trouble with Pitching Fellini 217

Chapter 33—Federico and Christina in New York. 227

Chapter 34—The Green One and the Pink One in L.A. 231

Chapter 35—You Exist Only in What You Do 237

Epilogue. 243

Acknowledgments

I would like to express my gratitude to the many people who saw me through this book, to all those who provided support, offered comments, allowed me to quote their remarks and assisted in the editing, proofreading and design.

I thank "You" for all your guidance.

To those who were on my personal and spiritual path; my "Oma" Felicitas Fuchs for holding the seed to my teachings and spiritual practice; to my parents, Heinz and Elisabeth for their values and discipline; to my daughters, Lily and Emma, for pure love and forever being closest to my heart; and special thanks to Eugenio Cappuccio for countless loving memories and to those who were on the path with me that lead me towards the moon and towards Tulum...

Geri DeMarlo, David Rifenbark, Giulietta Masina, Fiammetta Profili, Francesca Fabbri-Fellini, Andrea De Carlo, Maurizio Grimaldi, Sophie-Anna, Brinke Stevens, Tullio Pinelli, Vincenzo Mollica, Milo Manara, Countess Grifeo, Norma Giacchero, Roberto Benigni, Paolo Villaggio, Marcello Mastroianni, Luca Verdone, Vittorio Cecchi-Gori, Mario Cecchi-Gori, Riccardo Fellini, Magdalena Fabbri-Fellini, Franco Amurri, Meir Teper, Dr. Ava Cadell, Robert Evans, Van Greenfield, Robert Farber, Stanley Handman, Howard Wills, Jennifer Griffith, Caroline Rodehau, Verdine White, Jim Martyka, Linda Fulton, Paramount Pictures, the representatives of the Mayan Indian tribes. And to those who I might have failed to mention, thank you...

And of course, thank you Federico Fellini, The Green One.

FOREWORD

They were very special years and what happened from 1985 to 1993, even perhaps beyond, possibly marked with signs of something extraordinary was also to reoccur again in 2019, a year before the centenary birth of one of the greatest geniuses of cinematic art in the 20th century, Federico Fellini.

Those were roaring years, in which creativity and vitality, not without contradiction, had in this world an explosion of particular energies that permeated everywhere, at all levels, creating phenomenal variations of nature of which artistic, political, anthropological even planetary have left and continue to leave signs.

In those very special years, I had the good fortune of becoming the second assistant to the director Federico Fellini on his film Ginger and Fred, and for whom I had done some advertising posters of which Fellini incorporated into the film.

It was good fortune for a 23-year-old in love with cinema. But this event wasn't enough of a mark on my life. As always, thanks to the interception of fatal destiny which had already prepared me by allowing me to meet Fellini, and on that same route, I spotted 'her' again, the writer of this book. It was a prepared lunch during a break of mounting the film of Federico's even as I was continuing my work after the finish of filming, and during that moment of which I was struck by the woman in question.

Christina Engelhardt was beautiful, for an Italian guy. She was the prototype of an exotic woman to conquer, tall, blonde, with green eyes and if you add to this the fact that, yes she was also the esteemed friend of the Boss, Fellini, and had the attention of everyone at the table enchanted by her prestigious games; I looked at her with admiration and curiosity. Well, you can understand how a young boy with hormones and creativity galloping, a figure like hers could have a detonator effect equal to atomic. And without losing heart in front of the shock-wave of that beautiful female, me, Fellini's young assistant took the courage with all four hands and stepped forward.

So began our story that ended with a fabulous wedding on the 8/8/1988. I knew immediately that beyond that nice figure, Christina was a charming creature, sensitive, and mysterious, and as I began to piece together all the incredible stories that she and the others had told me of the strange events that occurred the year before in Mexico, with her, Fellini, Andrea De Carlo, Maurizio Grimaldi, in order to retrace the path of Carlos Castaneda.

Of course all of these events had to be investigated scrupulously and like a detective, I have to say they are absolutely true, verified and have happened. And it is on this basis, in 2019, I will be presenting at the Venice Film Festival, my film, "Fellini Fine Mai" (Fellini Forever) which also delves into those events, and are based on this book, Towards the Moon.

Christina having asked me to write a page for the foreword, I do so with enthusiasm, first of all, because there is a need for intellectually honesty in dealing with enigmatic mysterious material that uses great objectivity, but secondly, because I think that the elements of understanding 'this story' have yet to be pieced together.

As this incredible history has at its source, thanks to the will of Fellini, the very ingredients regarding making a film about the Mystery of Magic, where the potentiality of composing, writing and realizing, I believe, are still a reminder that we are only at the beginning of explaining a truly new, fascinating, and incredible story.

Eugenio Cappuccio, Director/Producer
Towards the Moon with Fellini and *Fellini Fine Mai*
Rome, 2019

INTRODUCTION

"I think of you often, dear friend, and after all that has happened, it is the least I can do. I'm still a bit shaken and confused, and of all this extraordinary and mysterious experience, your image is the most concrete, the most relaxing, the most solar."

– Letter from Federico Fellini to Christina Engelhardt, Nov. 6, 1984

It's time.

Over the last three decades, I have formed my own theories on what happened. I've pondered why I was involved in such an incredible experience and found some answers through my fascination with and studies of spirituality, theology, philosophy, and the everlasting question "What else is out there?" My thoughts have also been impacted by what's followed in the years after this bizarre, fantastical, and truly amazing series of events. For the most part, though, it's still elusive. It still leaves a myriad of unanswered questions, questions I still seek answers to even as I venture forth to write this book.

This is a tale of adventure and intrigue. It is at times unbelievable, at times terrifying, at times inspiring. It is *all* supernatural. It is a wild, action-packed journey deep into the unknown yet somehow, surprisingly familiar. It is a story of love, chaos, and growth. It is a calling to once again remind us that there is so much more beyond this plane of existence, so much more to see and experience if we just open our eyes, hearts, and souls. And if we are chosen. This story is deeply personal and necessary for me to share. I also believe this story is important.

As you will see from my writing, personal letters, documents, past interviews, photos, and more…what happened to me, to us, more than thirty years ago and in the years that followed is all completely true.

I was part of a mystical experience with the legendary Italian filmmaker Federico Fellini that would change not only how we would look at our existence as a whole but would also impact, intrigue and haunt us for the rest of our lives. It was foreseen that I would connect with this ethereal artist and go on an adventure. It was a prophecy given to me at another time and place. I was with Federico at a crucial point in his life, a time that saw his genius questioned, his artistic drive faltering and his need for a muse to rekindle his spirit and sense of purpose. We connected on our own unique level and I was an instrument, a healing presence by his side when the unbelievable occurred. I was part of his new life quest just as our experience together formed a new sense of purpose for myself. I was given a designation, a mission, a purpose beyond my own. I, like Federico Fellini, heard The Voice.

But why me?

Well, as you'll soon see…of course, me.

I have always been humbly open to the possibilities of something more. I am a devotee of the clairvoyant who comes from a bloodline of psychic mediums. I developed that gift at an early age and it fascinated me all my life. I've always believed in something bigger watching over me and guiding me, a God source of some kind. In my quest to understand more about that, I have also spent the better part of my life both honing my skills as a clairvoyant and studying ancient beliefs, sorcery, magic and ideologies of the world. I've studied Tarot, numerology, astrology, energy fields, I Ching, Ruins, Taoism and the other Eastern culture philosophies to further my understanding of the principles of knowledge. I've looked up to the ancient master teachers, including Jesus, Moses, Lao Tzu, Buddha, and Confucius, and I've hungered for theology in all forms.

In the early eighties, when this story begins, I was an international model and actress, a recent transplant to L.A. from

New York, who had moved based on a prediction that something more was awaiting me. I had traveled, experienced career success and made some high profile friends among the celebrity elite. Yet, I was at a crossroads, watching for a sign to tell me where my life was going to take me next.

I had no idea it would be the Yucatan. Nor did I know how that short but explosive trip would trigger a series of events that would affect the rest of my life.

Neither did "il Maestro." Yet, after decades of dabbling in the supernatural and building an award-winning and critically acclaimed legacy based on bringing his mystical visions to the masses, this particular experience would forever change Fellini...inspiring him, haunting him, frustrating him, and even humbling him.

As our story begins, Fellini has reached an artistic crossroads. His shared fantasies have awed audiences in Italy and around the world for years. Works like *I Vitelloni, The Nights of Cabiria, 8 ½, La Strada, La Dolce Vita, Satyricon, Juliet of the Spirits, Roma, Amarcord,* and so many more earned him his place among the titans of the craft and the visionaries of a generation. He was in a time where every director cites his work as an influence and all strive to not just be like him, but to BE him. He is the epitome of cinema, a living example to show why and how artists create art. His wildly exotic and luscious magic carpet ride adventures have cemented their places in eternity as contributions to not just art, but explorations of religion, freedom, fear, love, desire, and spirit. As I got to know Fellini, the man and the visionary, I quickly realized one everlasting truth about his films: He lived so he could dream and he dreamed so he could make films. He made these films so he could reveal one little truth and one little lie about humanity.

To say he was touched by something more would be an understatement. When we see what's produced by the great artists of any generation, part of what awes us is not just the talent and the creativity, but the *source* of where this creativity, this art, this statement of worldly relevance comes from. Is it God? The gods?

Or maybe it's an untapped part of the human brain that can only be accessed by a select, lucky few. Maybe it's both. The ancient Greeks, after all, believed inspiration would send artists into "furor poeticus." This translates to something like "the divine frenzy," where the artist would temporarily give up his mind to make room for the gods or goddesses to come through. For Christians, there's a belief that artistic inspiration comes from within our souls, tapped and guided by the Holy Spirit. Some believe it comes from past experience, from the artist's own journey and influential upbringing; just as Fellini's experiences during World War II and watching the circus and its uniquely outlandish characters come to town affected his perspective and his art. Some believe it comes from inherent generational struggles, feats and accomplishments. Others believe inspiration comes from a rare connection with nature and seeing what most cannot in the world around us. Still others believe inspiration comes from worlds, planes, realities *beyond* our own…and ultimately, that's where our story takes us.

As I became more involved with Fellini, I saw firsthand how his inspiration came from *all* of these sources. Fellini was not just open to multiple muses, he hungered for them, seeking them out wherever he could, even within the paranormal. He was not the first artist to act on counsel from unconventional sources, but he was perhaps the most open to it, at least of any recent generation. He was always searching, a Puppet Master pulling at the strings of reality and as you'll soon see, his search took him to some fascinating places.

Yet, in the early eighties, on the eve of his next great adventure, he was lost, even in the safety of his dreams. He found himself doing international commercials to earn a paycheck, waiting for the inspiration that now seemed to elude him and searching desperately for a producer that would be patient enough to look past his temperamental working reputation and help him bring his visions to the screen. Needless to say, il Maestro had never felt so tired and confused in his life. After a short string of failed launches, Fellini knew he had to redefine himself and he was trying desperately to figure out how. The muse, whatever the source, had touched him so easily before and now this visionary genius felt abandoned. While revered as a deity, on the surface, Fellini was elusive, an enigma to even those who knew him and celebrated him. But as I got closer to him, I saw vulnerability under the tough exterior and in those moments he opened himself up, seeking help from something greater.

That, I believe, is why The Voice came to him just before that fateful trip to Tulum. This is why Fellini, a few members of his inner circle and I were able to gain access to…well, you decide.

This story is about two very different people who meet and experience something extraordinary together that shaped the rest of their lives. Fellini and I have a meeting of fate's design in L.A. and soon find ourselves in Tulum, in the heart of the Yucatan, trying to track down the famous self-proclaimed shaman Carlos Castaneda as reflected in Fellini's graphic novel, *Trip to Tulum*. Along the way, we open a portal, giving in to The Voice, who quickly takes control of us, our relationship, and our path. After the trip, as we both try to make sense of what's happening to us, we know only that we are in this together. We have been told as much. The trip and this new presence in our lives lead to more Fellini projects (in a way). It also leads to frustration, confusion, and even terror as we continue to disappoint and anger The Voice, who constantly reminds us of the importance of our work.

All the while, as we work to appease its commands and we bear witness to its power, we seek desperately for an understanding of what exactly is happening. Could this be an elaborate and prolonged prank? Is this all being imagined, fueled by our choices, moods and experiences at the time? Or is The Voice truly what it tells us in its vague, cryptic messages? Is it in fact something bigger, something not of this world or dimension? The questions of "Who?" and "Why?" drive us close to insanity…and yet, we feel it chose us for a reason. That struggle of what to believe and how to work with our new circumstances while trying to truly judge their importance would define the next several years of our lives. They are questions that would haunt Fellini until his death. They would cause me to go on a decades-long journey, a metaphysical muse in a great search to seek understanding, including trips back to the Yucatan where it all began.

Towards the Moon with Fellini chronicles my unique relationship with Federico and our bizarre experience together in the later stages of his life. My time with Fellini was joyful. I spent a good portion of nine years very close to him, including a year following him with a camera that was eventually turned into an award-winning documentary directed by Eugenio Cappuccio with the same title of this book. From our first meeting on, we were a large part of each other's lives. Even with all of his accomplishments, he admired and appreciated me as a person. He showed me off to everyone, taking me everywhere, introducing me as family. Despite our deep love for each other, we never had a physical relationship…partially because we were told by The Voice not to cross that line. Instead, I served as a muse, a friend and his psychic consultant and he became a strong father figure. We were above all else, partners in an adventure that I will now share with you, leaving room for you to form your own thoughts on what exactly happened and why.

It's important for me to say again that everything you find in the pages of this book *happened.* This is not based on a true story. This IS a true story. Some of what you read you will find hard to believe. Now, after all this time, I still find some of it hard to believe. This is a supernatural story that I happened to share with a legendary artist. Once you see the details of that story, you will find yourself mystified.

I can see already that the main question I'll get from this is, "Why did it take you so long to write?" There are many, many, *many* reasons. One was out of fear, which, once you meet The Voice, you'll understand why. Another reason was the trouble I had processing the experience, especially after I lost my partner. I've also spent a good part of the past twenty years touring and promoting my film, and trying to form a life for myself as a business woman and mother, while also examining what exactly happened. I have been retracing my steps, seeking clarity and understanding of the whole experience in terms of what it meant at the time and what it means now. As for the question of, "Why now?" this book is part of that process and the timing just feels right. Honestly, the story is simply too compelling to keep to myself any longer.

Yes, it's time.

More than anything, it is my hope that you can simply enjoy this fascinating tale of the impossible and see that there truly is more out there. I want you to enjoy this story of a defining moment for one of the most dynamic, fascinating, and influential personalities in the history of the film industry told through the eyes of one of his closest confidants. I'm writing this book as part memoir, part mystery, and part examination of the beliefs we hold about higher powers, what else is out there, who we are, and where our inspiration truly comes from.

Many authors don't write their introduction until after they are done with the book, but I'm doing mine first as a sort of *mission statement*; a way to frame what I'm about to share and, more importantly, why. I am writing this first as a commitment to myself to finally go forward and do this, to share this incredible story once and for all. While Fellini is gone, I now have you along with me as I take this step forward. Thank you for wanting to share this adventure with me.

Now, grab my hand and let me take you towards the moon with Fellini.

Chapter 1

You Are Now Part of Something Important

The Voice came through the telephone and into Federico Fellini's ears, and there was instantly something unusual and concerning about it. There was a metallic ring to The Voice. It had no distinct accent, sex, tone. It was almost robotic, yet somehow more human than human. Though its words were clear, The Voice itself was distorted, as if coming through a machine from many miles, years, and dimensions away. Federico would tell me later, as we discussed what we would eventually call "You" and its mission for us, that he remembered in that first phone call, the first contact from this other presence, that he felt confused and even annoyed.

More than anything, he felt unsettled.

"You are about to start a great adventure. You will discover something about yourself. You are going to understand that there is more. There will be others with you and you will bring a message to the world."

Fellini *didn't* understand and his first impulse was to ignore this Voice and its cryptic yet prophetic message…even though it continued to call him. He was focused on his next project and this was an unwanted distraction that he was ready to write off. Then it spoke to him of private things: experiences, events, even translating his thoughts and emotions. It spoke to him of things Fellini had never shared, things so intimately personal that he dared never speak of them.

1

The Voice knew he needed to be convinced.

Yes, even Fellini, perhaps the most cosmically open and accessible artist of this or possibly any generation, a man who actively sought the divine, the supernatural, couldn't comprehend exactly what was happening to him, and more important, what he should do about it.

Like me, Fellini asked, "Why?" And while my past and my interests would quickly help me form an understanding of my role in this great adventure, the question of "Why?" would pull at Fellini throughout our experience together and beyond. It would be something he wouldn't quite ever be able to grasp and, at times, that confusion would deeply affect him. This was especially true when You would make demands that he either couldn't understand or got wrong…and You would show its disappointment. Fellini, a man with a tremendous ego who never shied away from self-importance, a man who proudly called himself The Puppet Master for his control over people, felt both possessed and humbled by The Voice.

You's visit, its reaching out to Fellini above all other artists now seems to make perfect sense. Federico Fellini was a highly influential man, an artist the world looked to and listened to, a man who built his reputation on speaking through "other" sources. He was open to his dreams, to the collective unconscious, celestial inspiration, the divine, and he created, produced, and shared the messages he received, whether he understood them or not. He was already considered a soapbox for the supernatural. He openly and faithfully accepted any powerful messages when they came to him. While he would never admit it, Fellini was extremely vulnerable in the sense that he *needed* these messages. These visions defined him. They were often the only thing that would balance his internal fire, his bombastic nature, his constant yearning for something greater that was often just beyond his reach.

"Our dreams are our real life," Fellini once said in an interview. He believed these dreams gave us our true moments of clarity, where the answers to the bigger questions could be found.

I would learn so much about Federico in our years together as collaborators. I would see how his focus could easily shift from one idea quickly to the next. He was notorious for getting bored with his films as soon as they were made. I would see his surly side and that quick, hot Italian temper, especially when dealing with producers, actors, and even fans and the media. "An interview is a halfway point between a psychoanalytical sitting and a competitive examination," he once said angrily...during an interview. I would see how charm and flattery could absolutely melt him, especially if it came from the lips of a beautiful woman. I would see how any hint of disrespect toward him would send him in a rage and if confronted, he would tear his accuser up, regardless of who could see or hear. I witnessed how protective he was of his reputation and his career and how quickly he would shut down if he felt either was being encroached upon, even by family. Fellini helped his brother Ricardo with his acting career by putting him in his first three films, but when Ricardo suddenly wanted to start directing on his own, Fellini shut him out and Ricardo's career as a director quickly fizzled to documentaries. And yet, I could also see how deeply and passionately he would *feel*. When an actor on the set of one of his films cited in a note Fellini's constant belittling of him as a reason he was going to commit suicide, it troubled the great director. I would also watch as Fellini treated tenderly those that he loved and needed the most...occasionally.

But of all these many sides of his personality, it would be this availability to the unknown, this devotion to the bigger questions, that would come to define not only Federico's life since he was a boy, but also our relationship, our adventure in the later part of his life, and the legacy he would leave behind.

Federico didn't speak much of his past or his upbringing. In general, he tended to focus on what was happening now, in front of him, rather than what had already happened. Still, he was greatly influenced by his past experiences; be it his modest childhood in small town Rimini off the Adriatic Sea, his strict Catholic upbringing and education, his discovery and fascination with the circus and its exceptional cast of characters (especially the archetype of the

3

classic clown Pierrot), his early studies and involvement with various political ideologies, his time working as a caricaturist and gag writer, his terrifying and intimate firsthand accounts of his beloved country's struggle as Mussolini launched Italy into World War II, his wife and life partner Giulietta and the loss of his only son Pierfederico just one month after his birth, and his rise into prominence in the Italian cinematic scene. Though he would often publicly deny it, all of these experiences would shape not just how he carried himself as one of Italy's most treasured artists, but also how he expressed himself and his visions in his films.

To break down and analyze both Fellini's growth and eventual international influence in the cinematic world as well as the stories behind his most famous films is a book in itself (and there are several that already exist). *I Vitelloni, La Strada, Nights of Cabiria, La Dolce Vita, 8 ½, Juliet of the Spirits, Satyricon, Amarcord*…these are just some of the films for which he won awards. There are so many more that were recognized by both critics and film aficionados years after their release (*Paisa, I Clowns, Fellini's Casanova, Intervista, Roma*, etc.). In the making of these films, there are legendary tales of conflicts with producers and famous actors, a mad genius developing his own style and often working without a script but with a clear vision in his head and his own renderings for storyboards, a group of devoted followers constantly struggling to understand and execute that vision, his ability to find beauty in the contorted, the grotesque, the absurd, studios rising to prominence and/or quickly falling based on his impulsive decisions, critical acclaim and critical hatred, accusations of immorality, sexual expression, the pushing of political agendas, censorship, banishment, and a host of awards it would take a wing of a home to hold.

Through it all, over the course of his grand and ever-fluctuating career, one thing remained constant and true and that was Fellini's dedication to following his dreams and visions. As such, his films' majesty was in their beauty, complexities, and evocative, surreal imagery. He once said, "My films are not for understanding. They are for seeing."

He sought anywhere and everywhere for understanding and the deeper meaning in these visions that would often haunt him. He knew they were coming from a place greater than this existence. He was titillated by the metaphysical world. He followed the teachings of Carl Jung, Rudolf Steiner and the psychology of the unconscious, studied I Ching, recorded and interpreted his dreams, took part in parapsychology, and even experimented with LSD. He would later study astrology, tarot, anything that could guide him through his visions and give him a grasp of who he was and what he was supposed to be doing on this plane and the next.

As such, we were truly destined to find each other. As he yearned, The Voice was also destined to find him.

At the time of You's intervention in our lives, il Maestro was floundering. It was 1984 and Fellini hadn't experienced a critical or box office success in nearly a decade, since *Casanova* (who some would consider a moderate success at best). He had a number of abandoned projects, once even walking off the set of a film, *The Journey of G. Mastorna,* mid-production because he had a dream that he himself would die in a plane crash if he continued to make a film about a plane crash with the survivors stuck in purgatory. With his reputation of going over budget, bickering with and sometimes abusing his actors, working without a script and blowing off his other studio responsibilities, Fellini had pretty much burnt every bridge with producers he had. In fact, at the time, Fellini found himself shooting commercials for products like Campari Soda, Barilla pasta, and generic wontons in Japan.

On a personal level, a book had just been released chronicling an affair he had with one of his mistresses, and his marriage was suffering because of it. A known Lothario, it was no secret that Fellini had a bevy of beauties, but he was still very devoted to his wife and didn't want to hurt her. The public reveal of the affair from this brief fling and his seemingly broken relationship with his muse greatly upset and frustrated Fellini, and he could feel the walls closing in. He was tired, confused, and he felt that everyone wanted a piece of him. He was also artistically blocked. He would dream of being lost at sea. The longer this went on, the more he believed that magic or something supernatural would be his only saving grace, a personal guide he needed to find to free him from his artistic prison.

That's when he got the idea to focus on Carlos Castaneda, thus triggering this unbelievable series of events. Federico came to the conclusion that making a film about magic and mysterious sorcerers would dispel the dark cloud he was under and Castaneda would be his answer. In early October, 1984, Fellini, who had been obsessed with Castaneda and his work on shamanism for the better part of a decade, had a chance to meet the reclusive yet illustrious anthropologist, author, and bringer of Yaqui Shamanism to the masses. Not much was known about Castaneda other than his radical thinking, undeniable literary talent, and objective curiosity about the system of Mexican shamanism, which he introduced to the Western world through his books. Castaneda's work also focused on the psychotropic effects of peyote and how humankind had only begun to tap into its own ultimate power. There was also a strange mythology surrounding Castaneda himself in that he was almost impossible to find, having buried himself deep in the Yucatan Peninsula in a mysterious place called Tulum. He managed to write a dozen books without ever giving an interview. No recent photographs existed where he could be clearly recognized. He rarely made appearances or even came out of hiding. He drew upon this experience of studying shamanism and living among the people of the Yucatan to write his first trilogy of books under the tutelage of "Don Juan," a master Yaqui sorcerer, whose very existence some questioned.

Fellini wanted desperately to acquire the rights to Castaneda's books to make a film. So when he got the call saying Castaneda was in Rome and wanted to meet, he jumped at the opportunity. It would be the first of three brief meetings that the two eccentrics were convinced had to happen. They seemed like a natural pair, a harmonious coupling that was destined for great things. When Fellini met Castaneda in his hotel room, he was greeted with a hug and the simple warm words,

"My dear friend, my dear friend." Castaneda was also convinced that the time was right for him to make a film…and there was nobody other than Fellini who could do it. In fact, he told Fellini that Don Juan himself had predicted this meeting. It was fate. It was a sign and Fellini believed it was destiny.

The plan was for Fellini to travel to Los Angeles for a follow up meeting and then to travel to some of the magical places in Mexico, more specifically, the jungles of Tulum, to scout for filming locations. Castaneda would be the catalyst for this trip to America, but in the end, he would have very little to do with the next stage of Fellini's incredible life. That would come from someplace much farther away than Tulum.

"*You must do what we tell you to do.*"

"I don't understand," Fellini said to The Voice.

"*You will…in time.*"

It was just days before his flight to America and Fellini was finally in a place where he felt confident about his path, as he did every time he was touched by inspiration. His recent troubles now seemed a distant memory for he was focused on this project and looking ahead to sharing this vision. He was confident the answers he was looking for were hidden deep in the ancient Mayan city in the Yucatan. He was ready. He didn't expect this phone call and he didn't need the distraction. Not now.

He would have little say in the matter.

"What do you want?" he asked.

"*We want you to do what you were meant to do.*"

Chapter 2

CHRIST-IN-AN-ANGEL-HEART

I was a key part of The Voice's plan, even if I didn't know it yet.

At the start, I felt very little fear. The first time the phone rang and I heard the crackling static on the other end, before The Voice even spoke, I instantly accepted my fate, my role in this greater, important adventure. I felt honored to be chosen, to be included in something more, even if I didn't fully understand exactly what was happening at the time. I was thrilled at the prospect of what I was sure would be the gift of clarity, new depths of knowledge, and cosmic understanding. If I'm being honest, this is something I had been waiting for my entire life. And it had been predicted. In a way, I had been trained for it. I was in tune, accepting, open and eager.

As soon as The Voice spoke to me in its foreign, cryptic tongue, I felt complete and I was prepared to do what was required of me.

I have always yearned to learn as much about who we are and why we're here as I possibly could. I have built a life exploring anything and everything that can give me answers. Like Fellini, I am fascinated by these bigger questions and the answers we can find if we just open up our hearts and minds. I look because I wonder.

I also look because of who I am.

I was born with a rare and special gift. I say that proudly, confidently, and humbly. I am a Creative Psychic Healer and I have been one since I was a very little girl. I can see and feel and sense and I am very good at what I do. There are many out there who don't believe in this power, and understandably so for there are many, many false "psychics" who pretend to possess a gift for their own personal gain. I am not one of them. I am blessed with an ability to read people and see things that others can't. There are not many out there like me and I don't say that to brag. I simply state it as a fact. Years of studying my craft, confronting pseudo-psychics, witnessing miracles, and helping literally hundreds of people has led me to understand that this is a blessing.

I can tap into the inner subconscious, into places others can't go. I focus on those feelings we all get, that feeling that tells you something good is about to happen or that maybe you just shouldn't go out tonight, and I pinpoint where they come from and what they mean. If I'm reading tarot, I see the patterns; they speak to me. Something in me opens up, a channel of sorts, that connects me to whoever I'm reading. The messages come loud and clear.

As such, I saw this whole experience with Federico as part of my plan, my path. My name is Babi Christina Engelhardt, or as I saw it: "Christ-in-an-Angel-Heart." From the moment I was a small child, this destiny to be a part of something greater felt marked out and prepped for me. All I had to do was open myself up and I started doing so when other little girls were still playing with Barbie dolls.

I was born in New Jersey. My parents had immigrated to America from Germany in the mid-fifties. They both grew up in and around Berlin during the chaos and moral and social destruction of World War II. A good part of their childhood was spent in bomb shelters and underground sewage tunnels. When my mother was just seven, a napalm bomb was dropped on her family home. She and my grandmother, who was eight months pregnant with two broken arms, had to push a cart with her injured siblings through the rubble to a hospital, hoping to find a doctor and fighting off Russian invaders. My father, like his father, was unwillingly drafted into Hitler's war at age fourteen. Though he didn't believe in Hitler or his cause, he was sent to the Black Forest to dig trenches with bullets flying over his head. What he remembered most was a decree from his superiors that nothing could be taken by the Allies, including themselves. My parents each had spent enough time in destruction, horror and misery and they wanted a better life so they both came to America. They would meet in New Jersey years after the war and formed a close bond over their horrific shared experience.

They brought the effects of that pain and a strong sense of resilience with them into adulthood, along with German discipline, a dose of disappointment for the actions of their countrymen and a fear of losing anything and everything they had built in their new life in America. They also brought an ability to survive, no matter the circumstances and they vowed to raise their children to be strong leaders who could and would do the same.

As such, my childhood was not the easiest. I am very close to my parents and have nothing but love for them. I know in my heart that they raised me the best they knew how, and they had the utmost love for me. They wanted to give me the best life possible, by preparing me the way they thought was best…and that was the problem. Because of their background, circumstances and experience, my childhood was strict and very tough. I could do very little without being admonished or worse. My parents were devoted to each other, first and foremost, which means they were always a team. While they were quick to admonish, they were never complimentary. Accomplishments were to be expected, not applauded. There were many, many expectations. They restricted what I did, *how* I did things, every aspect of my life… including what hand I wrote with, and more. Coming from a culture where, at the time, being left-handed was seen as a human flaw, they would tie my left hand behind my back to try and train me to use my right. I was regimented and it frustrated me in every single way. I could do little right, so I learned to maneuver myself around that. At the time, I accepted their strict discipline and my need to circumvent that as simply a way of life.

Still, I knew enough to know that other kids had more. I wanted a more loving family that did things together. All we ever really did was work and do chores, and every once in a while play games. We never took family vacations or even went on family outings, except for the yearly trips back to Germany to see my grandparents. It was a rather lonely upbringing in many ways, but one that helped build strength in me. It taught me the discipline to take care of myself.

Because I was German and there was still a lot of anti-German sentiment and fear, I was a loner at school who was often bullied. After I was introduced by the teacher on the first day of school as "the German girl," the kids started the never-ending teasing. "Babi's a Nazi! Babi's a Nazi!" The parents weren't much better. I was very shy and rarely tried to make friends, but even when I did, I was shunned by the parents who didn't want their kids hanging out with the German girl.

Beyond my heritage, I knew that I was different from everyone else. I had no real desire to tolerate the torments or the drama of childhood. Matawan, New Jersey just wasn't the place for me and I always felt like an outsider. I spent most of my childhood enjoying my long walks to and from school and befriending animals. I also developed a spiritual relationship with God, often talking to him when I was alone in the woods, at peace in my sanctuary. I was isolated, focusing instead on what I envisioned for my future. I had a life mission to make a difference and that was most important. I believed in something greater and that's where I turned my attention, focusing on a special power I felt growing

Well, it was actually a gift. When I was a little girl, I believed I talked to angels. I'm not talking about imaginary friends that most kids have. I had guiding spirits that I could feel; loving, peaceful creatures that would communicate with me. I also believed I could move things if I just concentrated hard enough. I *knew* I could see things…and that clairvoyance fascinated me more than anything. I was obsessed with it but I didn't know what it meant or how to handle/harness it. It was my "oma", or "grandma" who taught me what to do and set my course following in the footsteps of my ancestors.

My lineage is comprised of Northern European artists, craftsmen, and farmers. On my father's side, they were also strict and cold disciplinarians who I truly had no affection for; my brother Michael and I would hate going to visit them in Heidelberg, right on the Neckar River.

My mother's side was much more interesting as they long believed that they were gypsies who also practiced as psychics; the latter was kept and celebrated as a sacred gift. I found out very young that I was born into a long line of psychic mediums; my grandmother was a psychic, her grandmother, and her grandmother, and so on. For whatever reason, it skips a generation. My mother has absolutely no interest in it and truth be told, neither do either of my two daughters. But my grandmother essentially made her living with her gift and I admired that. Living in Germany, she grew up in a part of the world that constantly struggled with wars and shifting powers and the destruction that comes with it. Like me, she was a loner who clung to her grandmother and their shared ability to help her in difficult times. As she grew into herself, she practiced more and more and eventually used her powers to put food on her family's table by giving readings.

We would often go visit my oma near Hannover. Unlike my other grandparents', her house was a place of love. Set amongst gorgeous landscapes, there was always someplace to go, just as there was always family and friends dropping by. Oma was big personality in a petite body who just looked ancient and wise. She had black hair with a tinge of grey and even blacker eyes. She was very reserved and not one for small talk, but was always warm and welcoming. And yes, she was clearly a gypsy. For as long as I can remember, I was fascinated watching her read tarot cards. From the time I was four, I started pestering her about teaching me how to do it. Finally, after a few years of nagging, she gave me my first lesson. In just ten minutes, I picked it up and never looked back. My eyes were finally open. As I turned each shuffled card over, I saw pictures in my mind flash like a dream with vivid pictures. I saw past, present, future. I saw how deeply I could love and how deeply I felt for everyone. This gave me something to hold onto, a way to express myself and maybe even use my power for a greater cause. By the time I met oma again the following year, at age seven, I was practicing myself. I gave her a reading and she lovingly welcomed me to the "art of psychic healing."

From there, I started practicing all the time. I also started reading every book I could on the art of tarot, as well as palmistry, astrology, numerology, and even theology; anything that could open the gift inside of me. Before I even hit my tenth birthday, I was obsessed with finding a common thread that binds all the mysteries of the world together. My oma and I continued to grow in our relationship and I blossomed into the person I always thought I could be. Oma passed along words I would try to live by, words that would come into play much later in my life tale.

"No matter what you think is challenging or difficult, you can help others with this gift," Oma said. "You can make a positive difference in the world. It is our gift of many generations; from your grandmother, mine and those before. There are sacrifices, no matter what you do, but it is better to be of service to a higher good then to be self-serving."

I vowed to use my gifts to help others. Tarot was definitely my strength. There was a lady I gave a reading to when I was ten. She was an elderly lady from the neighborhood who hovered around me when my mother said I had a psychic gift. She asked if she could have a reading.

"Don't ask me," my mother said. "Ask Babi."

I was thrilled and quickly drew out my cards. I pulled her aside as I didn't want anyone else to hear because I instantly felt great pain in her spirit and knew it was no one else's business. Visions instantly started coming to me and I told her all I could.

"You have to stop taking those funny little pills as they're going to make you very sick."

"You should not blame or harm yourself because you chose not to have babies."

"Your sister will forgive you for taking her boyfriend years ago because he turned out to be a real 'bad guy' and it's better not to have raised his kids because he is in jail right now."

I watched as she broke down and cried. Everything this ten-year-old girl had told her was true. From that day on and to this day, my mother has to make a time schedule for my readings in her neighborhood. That was another beautiful aspect of this gift; it was the one thing my parents never once tried to control. They let me grow in this magic.

My upbringing, my family history, this generational gift that was passed onto me all played a major part in prepping me for what was to come. I see that now. My life was a purposeful journey, training to be ready for the amazing adventure I would go on with Fellini and to seek out what it would mean.

But this was just a part of the preparation. I had much more to explore. I had to open myself up artistically and take advantage of other gifts I was blessed with and see where they would take me. From my isolated home on a farm, I didn't think it would be very far. Little did I know what awaited me. Now I wonder what would have happened if I had not walked down that dirt road at that exact moment on that exact day.

Without fate, there is no story.

Chapter 3

YOU SHOULD BE A MODEL

High school proved no better for me socially...not that I was expecting anything different. I was a young psychic, who was spending her time studying tarot and world religions, living in a small New Jersey town going to school with a bunch of farmers.

They didn't understand me and I didn't understand them. Still, there were three things that happened during my high school years that had an impact on my life and this story. First, my abilities were really starting to grow into their own and I felt like I was mastering this psychic art. Second, I taught myself to drive and used some saved money to buy myself a car, which gave me some much-needed freedom. Third, I grew into myself physically. My freshman year, I was 5'8" and string-bean thin. I had long blonde hair, even longer legs and a face that would command attention. I soon realized that my looks could get me places.

They could also earn me pain and trouble.

I was thirteen the first time I was raped by a seventeen-year-old who was the local high school's starting quarterback. Flattered that someone so popular would talk with me, I allowed myself to fall into a dangerous situation and the worst happened. It wasn't long after that the same thing happened again, this time by a friend of my parents. Those incidents, along with some others and some equally painful treatment from boys I was interested in initially turned me off to the concept of sex at an early age. It was painful and embarrassing and I didn't want anything to do with it. But, it didn't turn me off from my sexuality and I quickly began to realize that my looks were another gift that could just possibly get me out of this existence and on to bigger and better things.

What would soon become an international modeling career started with a casual walk home from school. Honestly, it couldn't have come at a better time. By my sophomore year in high school, I was already reaching a breaking point. I needed to get out. Despite my feeling like an outsider, I had tried to be a "normal" farmland teenager. I studied hard, tried to make the occasional friend, worked a part time job, learned how to ride horses, got involved in extracurricular school activities like writing for the school paper and taking part in an art program, and even went out with the occasional boy. But none of it felt right. There was something bigger calling to me and I just couldn't figure out how to get to it.

My looks were the ticket. In high school, I submitted myself twice to the Miss New Jersey Pageant, making runner-up both times. As a side note, when I was nineteen, I would later win a pageant in Germany, giving me some vindication for the two losses. I'm not sure why I participated in pageants, as that sort of thing seemed completely out of my element, but nevertheless, at that early age, I began to learn the power of beauty. I was actually approached at age thirteen by Barbizon Modeling who offered to train me, but that was quickly squelched by my parents. But fate would once again bring the prospect of modeling back into my life a couple years later, and this time, with little left to lose, I would jump at the chance.

It was 1976. I started to walk up the long, dusty road after yet another uneventful day in the boredom of my daily country life. On this scorching summer day, the constant eerie silence of isolation was rudely and thankfully interrupted by a car roaring through a cloud of dust on what we called Gravel Hill Road. I gave the driver a slight glance as he passed, curious what he, what anybody, would be doing out here. I must have caught his attention because he stopped his car, skidding on the gravel, and backed up.

The first thing I noticed when he rolled down his window was his flashy diamond earring, which I think was meant to impress. It didn't.

"You should be a model."

That was the line he gave me. Yes, I was young and possibly desperate for a different life than what I had, something that could shake things up and help me get on my bigger path, that this flirty suggestion resonated with me.

"Sure, I've thought about it," I replied.

His smile won me over and he proceeded to tell me about the famous photographer Robert Farber, who he knew in New York City. He suggested that I should go see him. He gave me his number and made me promise I would call.

With that, I was on my way to becoming a model.

It made sense in a way. Other than the looks, I had a great deal of self-confidence and a very strong character. Plus, after years of being a loner, there was a great appeal to being seen and people wanting me. There was also the appeal of New York City, only an hour's drive but what felt like a million miles away.

I remember going to NYC with my father as a child; he had a business there. I marveled at the throng of people. It was exciting. It was different. It was a place where things happened. I set up an appointment and took that meeting with Robert. It was my first time adventuring by myself into the big city, but there was no fear, only excitement. I was brimming with confidence, ready to do anything to break out of the doldrums of a rural New Jersey lifestyle.

"At 5'8," you're not tall enough or skinny enough," he said. "And 120 isn't good enough. We want you at 110."

That's how I got my first taste of the real world of modeling. While disappointed, I was not going to be deterred. If dropping ten pounds was necessary, that's what I was going to do. I started dieting and for a short time, even developed a very unhealthy eating disorder. I knew better, but I was so desperate for a grander life than the one I had, that I was willing to make sacrifices, even dangerous ones.

I kept going back to New York and eventually I got introduced to photographer Andy Unangst, who would eventually become a very good friend. Andy was an extremely successful high end fashion photographer and he and I hit it off right away. Shooting with Andy, all my nerves went away and I fell in love with being in front of a camera…and how I looked on film. It gave me the confidence I needed and I started to build a portfolio. Not long after, I got an agent, met some other photographers, started getting sent out on occasional modeling gigs, and become part of the scene. It was an education in its own right to say the least, especially for someone as young as me, and I did it alone, without my parents' consent, knowledge, or restrictions.

I would balance school with my new career, trying to find time to do my homework after an afternoon shoot. I would work with photographers and hustle to find my own modeling jobs.

There was definitely a struggle for a time, but honestly, I found that modeling was easy; hanging with adults was what interested me. Kids my own age, especially in my school, didn't get me. I was bilingual and had already developed psychic talents. I did all the artistic things I could…reading tarot, writing, painting, and photography. I was working on my body to get it into model shape. Soon, some of my shoots started to appear in magazines like *Seventeen* and *Co-Ed,* and I had a couple publications do articles on my involvement in the business at such a young age. That stopped my classmates from any more teasing.

Soon, there was only one place I wanted to spend my time and that was the Big Apple. I wanted to meet more interesting, talented people and this was the place and the industry to do it.

New York is the most energetic city in the world, possibly more than Rome, Paris, etc. I absolutely loved NYC, still do. It's a city of people and connections, of doers. It's a city that can be extremely rewarding and extremely cruel. New York is where you can make anything happen and I still find that exciting. I continued visiting the city throughout my remaining years of high school and then moved there right after I graduated to pursue modeling full time.

While I had started modeling as the wholesome girl next door, my comfort in front of the camera soon opened me up more to my sexuality. Through my modeling, I had met several accomplished photographers who were nice and supportive like Bert Stern and Valentino, who brought out my sex appeal. I eventually ended up back at Farber's, this time with a little experience and confidence under my belt, and ended up shooting with him for one of his books. I even connected with the notorious George Senty, who I would stay with for a while, before he allegedly murdered another model, but that's a story for another time.

I completely fell into the scene. I befriended all the assistants, makeup artists and girlfriends, all of whom were always thrilled to get a psychic reading. I became friends with the other models too. Unfortunately, I also fell into some of the traps involved with the industry. I dealt with the pain of rejections, the manipulation from men in positions of power who wanted more from you, the constant hustle and need to build connections, the pressures of staying thin and to look your best and of course, the sexual experimentation and the drug use…in my case, diet pills. I also experienced some truly terrifying situations that went beyond the typical sexual harassment, including being kidnapped and briefly held by a Middle Eastern prince who was obsessed with me before I was able to make an escape!

Luckily, in general, I was smarter than most and was able to keep most trouble at bay, focusing more on the fun I was having. I loved going to the Roxy roller skating rink and skating with the wild Bohemian artists, dancing to disco music at Studio 54 with the likes of Mick Jagger, Margaux Hemingway, Andy Warhol, and more, and noshing at Elaine's for unbelievable food and the constant chance of meeting even more celebrities. I could fill another book with stories of celebrities and notorious personalities I met, worked for, partied with, and sometimes dated during my modeling years and beyond, including Robert DeNiro, Woody Allen, Mia Farrow, Sophia Loren, Christopher Walken, Orson Welles, Adnan Khashoggi, Richard Northcott, Julio Iglesias, Stephen King, Bill Malinchak, Jeffrey Epstein, and on and on. One I was particularly close to was Olivier

Chandon, the world renowned race car driver, heir to the Moet de Chandon champagne empire and notorious playboy. We dated for a while and got very close before a tragic accident on the track during a private practice session took his life.

Despite all the roller coaster excitement of this new life, I also took my career very seriously. I was in hyper-drive and very focused and disciplined on doing my best in this business. I did a lot of teen magazines, the *New York Post, Mode Magazine, Allure,* books, articles, and later even toyed with the idea of posing for both *Penthouse* and *Playboy,* which I tested for but didn't do. Over the course of my modeling career, I traveled to Paris, Rome, London, and multiple cities in my ancestral homeland of Germany. I was featured and written up in publications all over the world. I soon found myself in the elite models inner circle with the likes of Christie Brinkley, Janice Dickinson, Nastassja Kinski, Carol Alt, and many more.

It was a wildly exhilarating time, especially when I decided to parlay my modeling career into a chance at breaking into the world of acting. Acting made sense to me for a number of reasons. First of all, astrologically, Neptune, Mercury, and Mars conjunct in my fifth house of creativity and sexuality which means I'm a born performer. If astrology isn't your cup of tea, I also had a big, open personality that had been trapped for so long and was just waiting to break free. I wanted to express myself, my deep emotions, and my spirit to anyone who wanted to watch. The idea was so thrilling to me. Plus, I had been told by many photographers that despite my success as a model, I had more of the actress *look!*

Suddenly I found myself doing extra work, booking the occasional small part and studying with two of the craft's all time giants, Stella Adler and Lee Strasberg. The number of A-list stars who studied acting under their tutelage is staggering. I was repped by industry mainstay agent Richard Davis, who had discovered Grace Kelly, Yul Brynner, Yves Saint Laurent, and countless others. I met and befriended the legendary Italian film director Alberto Lattuada, who tapped me as his next discovery years before I even met his respected colleague, Fellini. In fact, for a short time, I was in the running to play a career-making role as Kitty in a major production of *Anna Karenina* with Alberto and Sophia Loren before they disappointingly went a different direction.

Still, I found moderate success as an actress in New York, appearing in decent roles in a handful of films and a featured extra in several more, but nothing compared to my modeling career. Still, I was having the time of my life. Beyond that, New York and its streets packed full of the most interesting personalities on the planet gave me a chance to truly stretch, hone and master my true talent.

As I pursued modeling and acting, I kept focused on my training as a psychic. I belonged to the East West Spiritual Center as a psychic medium in a private channeling group. I would participate in tests that opened up my third eye and tested my abilities. I gave readings anywhere and everywhere I could, including in both my modeling and celebrity circles, and developed a reputation as a go-to medium in New York. I found my inner voices spoke louder and clearer to me as I grew and my clients were amazed at what I could uncover, in terms of past secrets, hidden desires, and potential futures.

The years I spent traveling to and eventually living in New York were truly some of the greatest of my life. And yet, toward the end of my time there, I was unsettled. There were several reasons, but mainly it came down to a very frustrating relationship with a world renown director and personality.

At least that's what I thought. Turns out there were bigger forces at play.

Photograph by Valentino—Babi Christina starts her modeling career

Chapter 4

My Own
Harmonic Convergence

In the summer of 1984, just as I was unknowingly about to switch up my eventful life in New York, I started hearing word of the Harmonic Convergence, a global spiritual celebration to mark a major moment foretold by our ancient ancestors. The event, led mainly by New Age author and artist Jose Arguelles and The Global Family, would be a worldwide shift in consciousness as anybody and everybody would be encouraged to pray, chant, dance, meditate, sing, etc. in an effort to bring about, through a global human connection, the ever-fleeting goal of prosperity and world peace. The event itself wouldn't take place until 1987, at a point of importance in not just the legendary Mayan calendar, but also in the alignment of the planets. In 1987, on specific dates that were highly debated, all the planets would be aligned into three consecutive signs (Scorpio, Sagittarius and Capricorn). When it finally did occur, when mankind took part in the Harmonic Convergence, the results were less than we had hoped for, and yet, the real power was in the movement itself, what was achieved in terms of unity and spirit. That momentum started in 1984.

In that same year, just as the planets began their long trek to take their positions and humanity started thinking about the impact we could make as a collective and a feeling permeated that something important was going to happen, my life was forever altered, a stage was set, and I was prepped for my role in a cosmic story.

Geri DeMarlo was my guide.

In my time in New York, I became friendly with a model named Lourdes at a casting call. I told her I read tarot cards and did astrology and she said the best psychic she ever met was Geri, who lived on 57th Street, across from the famous Russian Tea Room.

Before I could even open my mouth at our first meeting, she read me.

"Ahh, you read cards and astrology too," she said, not asking.

We hit it off immediately.

Geri was an eccentric, magical woman. She was maybe four feet tall and very old and wise-looking, the epitome of a gypsy psychic. She was a foul-mouthed spitfire who was very caring, but didn't suffer fools and she could knock you off your feet with her wit. She sensed a lot about me immediately and we began a very close friendship; I referred to her often as my psychic mama. Over the next few years, we read for each other, and though our age difference was quite large, she accepted and respected my talents. I told her almost everything– things I didn't even tell my own mother. As for the things I *didn't* tell her or things yet to come, well, Geri's readings were never wrong. She could, in detail, predict what was going to happen next and how to approach those situations. Geri also scolded me if I didn't listen to her, whether it was getting rid of people around me she didn't like or reminding me I had a destiny of success. She knew the troubled and troubling men I met and was attracted to, the false friendships with people who used me, and the important work that was ahead of me!

That's why she kicked me out of New York.

I should back up because this all happened (at first, at least) because of a man. A very famous man, with whom I would have a steamy, scandalous, and life-changing relationship during my late teen years in New York.

I'm talking about Woody Allen.

I first met Woody at Elaine's while I dining with some of my friends. I saw him from across the room of the restaurant and was captivated by him, and I could tell he had noticed me as well. I had a

Geri DeMarlo as a dancer with Sammy Davis Jr., circa 1950s.

lot of respect for Woody as a director, and feeling brazen, I decided to try to and get to know him better. I wrote a note on a cocktail napkin and dropped it on his table. It read:

"Since I'm sure you've given plenty of autographs, I thought you should have mine. Wishing you all the best, Babi Engelhardt."

Folded up inside the note, I included my phone number and sure enough he called. A few days later I went on a first date with Woody, which consisted of talking, playing chess, and watching the Knicks together in his penthouse suite. The next time we made love. That started a relationship mainly built around me going over to his place for the occasional rendezvous.

Being so young and enamored that someone of his status would take interest in me, I fell deeply in love and naively thought we were soulmates. I was completely blind to how Woody viewed and used me, even after he introduced me to his other lovers, including Mia Farrow. It wasn't that he ever really mistreated me, he just never really saw me as anything other than a sexual partner, regardless of what he would tell me in our more intimate moments. I craved so much more from him. Our "relationship" was off and on for my entire time in New York. All the while, I thought I could be his muse, that I could inspire and all the while, I grew increasingly more frustrated by his indifference and seemingly lack of care or interest in my well-being. I inevitably couldn't help feeling used and being so young, I struggled with it emotionally, and tried to walk
away.

I also felt I was due for a change, for the next great adventure. I found myself looking harder and harder for a sign. It came in the form of Geri DeMarlo…and I heard it loud and clear. I had gone to visit her, unsettled about the disillusioned relationship with doubts and confusion about my place not just in New York, but this life as a whole. It's funny how even powerful psychics such as myself still need others to read what's going on in our lives. We open up our abilities for others, not ourselves. It's like psychic surgery, and no surgeon in any field ever operates on themselves!

Geri simply sat and listened to me vent, again. Then, she unleashed hell.

"It is time for you to leave!" she said.

I was perplexed at the sudden outburst.

"What do you—"

"No! Enough of this. You must leave New York."

Now, I was completely stunned. She didn't give me a chance to speak.

"You must leave this city and its useless love affairs that only bring you pain and sorrow. Enough. You must go."

Here she paused, only slightly, staring directly at me like she had dozens of times in the past. She was opening her talents up to me, allowing her voice to speak to her about what I should do. She was reading. It lasted just seconds, but what she said next would change my life forever.

"You have to move to Los Angeles."

Geri hated Los Angeles.

"And you have to be there by October 20th."

"Why?" was all I could ask, my head still reeling.

"You are going to meet someone. A famous Italian director. You will then live in Rome."

"WHAT?!"

"And you are going to be part of some—you are going to hear a voice that will tell you what to do."

"A voice?" I asked, having a hard time understanding and accepting what she was telling me. "From who?"

"I don't know, perhaps from fucking outer space."

She said it as nonchalantly as if it would be the voice of my father or a friend or the mailman.

"The heavens are soon going to open up for you to find your path," she said and suddenly I could see in her eyes that she was frantic. "But you have to go. You have to be out there by the 20th."

"But…I don't…my life is…"

She practically threw me out of her apartment.

Geri DeMarlo in her 80s.

"NO!" she screamed. She had never done that. For the first time in our relationship, I couldn't read her. I couldn't understand what was happening. All I knew is that she was adamant. "GET OUT! GO NOW! YOU MUST LEAVE!"

She actually pushed me toward the door, even as I tried to ask more questions. She didn't want to hear them. She didn't want to hear anything, not anymore. She had heard the only voice that mattered to her, the voice that made her who she was and its message was loud and clear. I had to go. I had to be in Los Angeles by October 20th for the next chapter of my life, perhaps the most important chapter, to start.

Geri was one of my most valued friends and a powerful psychic. Geri was never wrong.

Within a few weeks, I was driving across the country to start a new life, already wondering what October 20th, 1984 would bring, wondering if this meant there would be a harmonic convergence in my own life and how that would fit into the bigger picture. And that is where this story truly begins...

Chapter 5

It Begins in the City of Angels

"Are you okay?"

I had pulled over to the side of the road, leaving the BMW idling. We were somewhere in the deserts of Southern California, near Joshua Tree. I knew we were getting close, but I just needed a break. At certain times on this trip, it felt overwhelming. I had, after all, just completely thrown life as I knew it by the wayside, basically on an astrological whim. I had only taken that which I could fit in my car... along with a lot of fear of the unknown. I believed in my fate, in the signs I was given and mainly in Geri. Still, I was young and now I was without any sense of comfort, security or expectation.

"I'm just exhausted," I replied. "I need a minute."

David was a very patient man, my neighbor, a good friend, almost more of a big brother. I had known him since I was fourteen and we had been very close, even if he was a little older. David was also a highly successful drug dealer and was loaded with cash. When I told him I was going to move to L.A., he was very sad to see me go but very supportive, even offering to buy me a car...as long as it was a BMW ("A German girl needs a German car!"). He also offered to drive out with me to make sure I got there safe. In later years, I would hear that he eventually got caught for his dealings and served a stint in jail. Like so many others who make up our lives, we lost touch, but I will always remember his support on that trip, his patience for thousands of miles as I questioned my decision.

"Okay, I'm ready."

We pulled away, hitting the last few miles before L.A. and a new life that revolved around a very particular date and high, unbelievable expectations. A few more miles for me to look for signs that I was doing the right thing.

One observation about driving for days straight from sun up to sun down, only stopping for gas, meals, and restroom breaks, is it not only exhausts you and makes you irritable…it can also open you up to possibilities. All you have to do is look or get lucky depending upon what you believe.

We arrived in L.A., driving down one of the only streets I had heard of and visited in my two prior brief work trips to the City of Angels…Sunset Boulevard. I had no idea where I was going or what I was looking for. I knew I needed to find an apartment immediately but I didn't even know where to begin looking. For as resourceful as I normally was, I had come here completely unprepared. The exhaustion was now getting unbearable. I pulled into the parking lot of the French Hill Apartments, next to the legendary Comedy Store and the former House of Blues. Fully ignoring the "Parking for Tenants Only" sign, I pulled into the empty space marked #13 and got out to stretch, both my legs and my mind. It was October 1. I had just under three weeks to get myself settled here before this life-changing event was supposed to happen and I had no plan. What was I going to—

"Hey, you can't park there!"

The man behind the gate startled me. I just blurted out the first response that came to my mind.

"Yeah, well no one has apartment thirteen!"

He paused for a second.

"That's right…you here to see it?"

"Yes," I replied, feeling like I had received the first sign in days. The apartment, *my* apartment was large, sunny, beautiful and fully furnished. My life in L.A. was about to get under way. The exhaustion started to ebb and with it came excitement and sense of something important.

***

With each passing day, Fellini became more and more eager to embrace the artistic inspiration he believed he would find in Tulum. Later on in our adventures, he would tell me that he once thought this would be his most important film. He was convinced that this project would pull him from both his personal and artistic funk. While he was still unsure and terrified of The Voice, he was beginning to realize that it was not going away. Fellini believed it was playing a large part in sending him to the Yucatan. In fact, he wondered if The Voice wasn't Don Juan himself. Regardless, all signs, external and internal, were leading Fellini to Tulum.

He arranged a meeting with Castaneda in L.A. for late October, which was to be followed by a trip to Tulum and another meeting.

Fellini had been to L.A. before, including a very memorable trip in the late fifties, where he was supposed to attend the Oscars. In fact, some say his enigmatic reputation began to form during this trip when he immediately disappeared upon his arrival. Rumors swirled as to what the future master of Italian cinema was doing during his lost forty-eight hours, but most say he fell under the spell of Hollywood, hitting the jazz clubs, surfing, and shacking up with a local actress. He never really talked about it. But, by coincidence or not, that trip marked a change in Fellini's filmmaking style as well and the legend grew.

One thing I would learn, everything Fellini did was epic.

As he prepared for his trip to America, he became more obsessed with Castaneda and his mythical shaman guru, especially with the book *The Teachings of Don Juan.* Castaneda's work resonated with him as did the powerful beauty of Tulum, a site Fellini had almost once used for his film *City of Women* just a few years earlier. With his obsession came his trademark enthusiasm.

But that excitement was tempered with both annoyance and fear of the continued calls from The Voice. The calls followed him everywhere he went and The Voice continued to reveal intimate secrets and details of his life to him. These calls were physically draining Fellini. He would shiver and sweat every time the phone rang. He found himself short of breath and unable to speak. Whenever the call would end, Fellini felt as if he couldn't stand, as if he had aged years in just minutes. The Voice was often cryptic in its messages, yet Fellini believed everything it said was continually propelling him to Tulum.

That was confirmed when The Voice started to round out his traveling party.

Fellini had told a very influential partner in his life about The Voice—Tullio Pinelli. The prolific screenwriter had worked with Fellini on a number of his greatest projects, including *I, Vitelloni, La Strada, La Dolce Vita,* and *8 ½*. Fellini and Pinelli met at a newspaper kiosk in the late forties and instantly connected when they started talking of creative ideas, political affairs, and the supernatural. They were both visionaries and Pinelli was the rare breed that could help Fellini put his visions onto the page. Fellini confided in Pinelli about The Voice, but he too was skeptical, also wondering if il Maestro was a victim of an elaborate hoax or if he was losing his grip on reality.

Fellini stubbornly insisted on the reality of The Voice and its mission and tried to convince Pinelli. He wanted Tullio to make the trip with him, but Tullio had other responsibilities and couldn't leave. He also warned Fellini of the dangers of falling too much in his obsession with this Voice and with Castaneda. Even a man who had built a career off of Fellini's eccentricities and outlandish visions was worried about this project and where Fellini appeared to be headed.

That is, until Pinelli too heard from The Voice...but more on that later.

Fellini still wanted others to go with him so he turned to another writer he had known and collaborated with, the celebrated author Andrea De Carlo. Fellini loved the young writer's novel *Uccelli da gabbia e da voliera* (*Cage and Aviary Birds*) and had brought him on to assist with his film *And the Ship Sails On*. De Carlo had also recently made a short film about Fellini's process with his actors called *Le face di Fellini* (*The Faces of Fellini*). De Carlo was enamored with Fellini and instantly agreed to make the trip.

Next, Fellini turned to another friend, famed producer Alberto

Grimaldi, who was best known for his work on the Sergio Leone spaghetti westerns and the acclaimed *Last Tango in Paris,* as well as Fellini's *Satyricon.* Grimaldi was a long-time partner and confidant of Fellini…and sometimes even a personal savior. Alberto had helped Fellini both with his financial responsibilities and his reputation when he had impulsively shut down the production of his film *The Journey of G. Mastorna.* Fellini didn't feel comfortable around many people, but he did with Alberto. Grimaldi also couldn't make the trip, but he set Federico up with his son Maurizio who lived in L.A. and was thrilled to play a role in the great Fellini's next adventure.

It was in Los Angeles that Fellini lost all doubt that The Voice was not of this world. It was upon his arrival that it became more than just a Voice on the phone; it became an actual presence. It was at Los Angeles International Airport that he would witness the first of two strange and unusual events that were meant as a sign of proof of You's existence to Fellini. He was getting closer to his mission now and The Voice wanted to make sure there was no doubt. When Fellini would tell me of these two events later, I was initially skeptical. I perhaps would not have believed it if his companions hadn't witnessed the same events and offered the same account or if I hadn't eventually heard from The Voice and experienced You's power as well.

At LAX, as Fellini was about to get into a car to leave, he was approached by a stranger who looked as if he was in a trance.

"Federico Fellini?" the man asked, his voice barely audible and his eyes unfocused, as if he were gazing at something far away.

"Yes?" Fellini answered annoyed at the intrusion but curious as to what was happening with the man.

"I have something for you." The man pulled out an envelope from within his jacket pocket and handed it to Fellini. As soon as Fellini took it from his hands, it was if the man was jolted back to reality. His eyes focused and he looked around, taking in his surroundings.

"Where am I?" he asked weakly and Fellini told him he was at the airport.

"In Los Angeles," Fellini said.

"How did I get here? The last thing I remember I was at the airport in San Francisco…and now…I'm…"

With that, the man wandered off, visibly upset and confused. He didn't give Fellini a chance to question him further. All he could do was examine the envelope, which felt empty to him. He tore open the envelope and out dropped a stamp-sized piece of fabric, nothing else.

"Oh, it matches the color of your hat," De Carlo said.

Fellini removed his signature fedora and examined it inside and out. It did, in fact, match the color and pattern. Upon closer inspection, he found a stamp-sized hole cut out of the interior. Fellini was never without this hat. How anyone or anything could have taken this hat and made the incision was beyond him. The Voice would later claim responsibility.

Later, at the hotel, the guests would find a piece of paper that had been slid under the door, which was physically impossible; there was no apparent gap. When they looked down the hall, they saw no one. It looked like a regular sheet of paper, blank on both sides. But when they held it up to the light, they found a watermark of sorts inside the fibers of the paper, a symbol that they couldn't understand. At this point, Fellini rid himself of any skepticism and he knew he was in for the most unusual adventure of his lifetime. However, the message itself confused him.

"Be wary. You are looking in the wrong direction. We are helping you, but be careful. Proceed with caution."

This jolted Fellini who was convinced that he was doing exactly what he was supposed to be doing for himself *and* for The Voice. He was so convinced that he ignored the note, assuming it was a mistake or some type of miscommunication. It wouldn't be the first time, especially at the beginning, that Fellini's ego overruled his better sense of judgment.

In L.A., that first night, Fellini and his entourage had another short meeting with Castaneda, who laid out plans for the group to go on a sort of spiritual scavenger hunt to some of the places of his stories. In later years, members of this entourage would declare early skepticism of Castaneda, who seemed like he was playing a game to impress Fellini. But il Maestro was eating it up, eager to go on this adventure, hoping it would enlighten him to something greater. That was, after all, his eternal quest.

Fellini felt ready and excited. Later that day, the phone rang, setting in motion the actions that would bring us together.

"Your group is almost complete. But there are still others that must join you. Tonight, you will go out and one from your entourage will bring a dancer. She will bring a woman. That woman will play an important role."

Fellini was confused, as always, but after what he had witnessed since his arrival, he was beyond questioning The Voice. He was ready to comply, the Puppet Master now just a puppet. To further add to the confusion, The Voice told Fellini that he would sleep with this dancer. As to why, again, The Voice offered no answer.

Maurizio offered a possibility for this new member. A couple months before, he had met a ballerina who, to respect her wishes for privacy, we will call Sybil. The pair had flirted and gone out once or twice and Maurizio had bragged to her about his recent connection with Fellini. He called her about the dinner and she was very excited to be invited…until he told her about sleeping with Fellini.

"That's not going to happen."

"Well, then find us somebody who will."

Sybil and I had met before in New York. Though we had a very indifferent and sometimes rocky relationship, we shared a mutual friend in a woman named Collette who was an assistant for Ken Marcus, one of *Playboy's* top photographers. Based on the nature of the request, Sybil thought Collette might have some suggestions.

"What about Christina?" she said. "She's always up for an adventure."

That's when I got the phone call.

***

I spent the month of October getting myself acquainted with my new home, learning about my neighborhood, looking for a modeling and acting agent, establishing myself as a tarot reader, going out on gigs, and connecting with colleagues and friends I had living in the city. After the compact and comfortable hustle and bustle of New York, L.A. seemed so lonely, big. and spread out to me. I was still pining for my last relationship and my love for the East Coast. I didn't know the hot spots here, the hip people, or what was happening underground. I was feeling lost, trying to focus on the pending date of October 20. I took in a friend for a roommate, a model and actress named Brinke Stevens, who would become a notable "scream queen." She would prove a wonderful confidant.

I was really struggling, torn between my excitement and the anticipation of something new and unusual and my questioning how it would happen and how I would react. I was a person of great faith, but as the days went on, this whole experience felt unsettling. I wondered if Geri was wrong, if I had been careless and if this wasn't meant to be.

The morning of October 20, I refused to leave the apartment, more specifically, the room with the phone. I woke up after having not slept very much and tried to get a *sense* of the day. It didn't feel any different and that in itself concerned me. I had come to rely on these feelings. I had moved here on these feelings. I had surrounded everything in my life on these feelings…and I felt nothing.

The morning past, no phone call.

The afternoon, no phone call.

Around 5 p.m., Brinke tried to get me out with some of her friends, but no, I couldn't leave. Still though, no phone call. This was ridiculous. This was insane. This was a mistake. This was—

The phone rang at 6:35 p.m. It was Sybil, a voice I didn't expect to hear. In the years since, Sybil and I have formed a friendship. But, back then, due to a number of misunderstandings, jealousy, and harmful mistakes, we really didn't care for each other…a point she made as soon as she called.

"Look, I don't like you and you don't like me, but I have to go to a dinner tonight and can't go alone. It's with a famous Italian director. I am supposed to bring a female companion and I've asked every single girl I know. No one can make it. So even though you are on the bottom of my list, I'm asking you if you can come."

I ignored her tone, her implications, her attitude, her bitchiness. All I heard was "famous Italian director" and I said yes. She didn't know what I knew and I didn't care how this meeting was to take place. This was what I was told was going to happen. She told me a car would be by to pick me up at eight.

"I will be ready!"

But there was no way I could prepare for what came next.

Chapter 6

THE PINK ONE
MEETS THE GREEN ONE

He was polite, shy, gentle, and soft-spoken.

That first night would be the only time in my life that I would ever think Federico Fellini was polite, shy, gentle, and soft-spoken. Over the course of our relationship, I would see the charm, the childlike curiosity, the constant flirtation, the temper, the yelling, the angel and the devil that sat on his shoulders. I would see many layers that made him truly one of a kind. But that first night, as he sat next to me in his iconic hat and tweed jacket, I saw a handsome, elegant, and mysterious charmer who had a tender side and a fascination with the moment to moment movement of the world.

When I climbed into the back seat of the black stretch limo and shifted over next to Fellini, I was pleasantly surprised. I wasn't expecting him. Sybil had told me that we would be dining with the Italian director Franco Zeffirelli. As soon as I got into the car, I saw this wasn't Franco. This was someone very different, someone with whom I was very familiar and I could have only hoped to meet. I was so excited that I was overly bubbly and cheerful.

"Hello, I'm Federico Fellini," he said.

I could tell that he was instantly appraising me as well. He was wondering if I was the woman that The Voice had spoken of, the all-important piece to this puzzle. I'm sure he was also trying to assess if I or Sybil or both would sleep with him. Andrea, Maurizio, and

Sybil were in the car as well and I could instantly feel tension from them, that I was an outsider to this group and that I was only there because of The Voice, something they didn't understand.

To help break the ice, I focused on Fellini and told him about my trips to Italy. I said we had a friend in common and mentioned Alberto Lattuada by name, and that I had known him since 1979. Alberto had helped Fellini in his salad days, co-directing a movie together and liked to call him his discovery. Fellini was amused by me and my attempts to flatter him.

"It's a great honor to meet you in person," I said, nervous and smiling.

He laughed a lot on the way to dinner and I instantly felt a connection.

As the five of us sat at Trader Vic's, a Beverly Hills mainstay, that connection grew, despite the efforts of other members of Fellini's entourage.

"Mr. Fellini, I should tell you that Christina does astrology," Sybil said. It was meant to be condescending, and I was unsure as to why the person who invited me was so upset that I was there. Not that I cared...I just found it curious.

"Oh, I love astrology!" Fellini replied, excited.

Now my curiosity was definitely peaked.

"But Mr. Fellini, she also does tarot!"

"Oh, I love the tarot! Do you also toss the coins for I Ching?"

Sybil had no idea that Fellini had such similar fascinations and I wondered if she knew who he was or had ever seen any of his films.

"Every day I toss the coins," I replied, beaming with pride. Now I had all of Federico's attention. Trying to regain her footing, Sybil showed off the crystal she carried in her purse as a way to show her spirituality. I pulled several out of mine and gave one to each person at the table.

"Now we're all spiritual," I said.

The whole table laughed...minus one.

Once the dinner finished, they drove me back to my apartment. I panicked. We had a great time, but there was nothing of real meaning that had happened. Surely this couldn't be it, I thought. Surely there was something more that I moved out here for, something that was yet to happen. I couldn't let this evening end…not yet.

"Would you be interested in coming up to my apartment and watching my slideshow?"

I was a bit of a hobbyist photographer and I had compiled images from my trips around the world. It was a long shot, but I hoped Federico might be interested and it seemed like a harmless enough request.

He instantly answered yes, perhaps remembering You's suggestion that he was to sleep with one of tonight's guests. Andrea and Maurizio weren't as enthusiastic but they were willing to go wherever Fellini wanted. Sybil, on the other hand, told the limo driver to take her home.

"A ballerina has more important things to do than look at silly pictures," she declared. With that, gratefully, she was gone.

We gathered comfortably in my living room on my white sofas. I put on some music (George Winston served as a suitable score), turned the lights off, hit the projector switch, and there against the white wall, eight feet tall were images from Europe, America, the Caribbean and eventually Mexico.

More specifically, Tulum.

"Have you heard The Voice?"

I smiled as Fellini jumped up and yelled out his mysterious question. The smile quickly dropped from my face as I saw a look of fear on his. He was suddenly sweating and looked very uncomfortable, as if I had reminded him of something painful.

I told him I didn't understand.

"These pictures of Tulum. This is where we are going, where we are being lead. This is where The Voice wants me to go."

I told him that I had visited Tulum because I was interested in shamanism and the ancient mysteries as well as the works of Castaneda.

"Castaneda?! Did The Voice reveal itself to you too? Have you heard it? What did it tell you?"

I was utterly confused but tried my best to explain to him that I had my own *inner* voice that I listened to for help with my readings and channeling and that voices come in many forms, but that I didn't understand what he meant by this specific Voice.

Andrea and Maurizio sat silently, letting this scene unfold before them. They had witnessed Fellini flustered and frustrated before, especially since The Voice had become part of this journey.

"You have to have heard The Voice," he insisted, now pacing back and forth in my living room. Occasionally he would look up at the slide, as if it were calling him and reassuring him that I was a willing part of this. "You know. You know of our mission."

I again said I didn't but that I would like to learn more. Feeling like the moment was right, I also finally confessed about Geri's prediction and why I moved to L.A. Perhaps it was a bold move on my part, but like him, I was seeking an answer.

"Goodnight, Christina," Fellini said suddenly. Just like that, in a flash, they were gone.

I sat there scratching my head, wondering what had just happened and what it all meant.

"A slideshow?" I said to my now empty apartment. "I left New York and moved to L.A. for a slideshow?!"

It didn't make sense. There had to be something more. I turned to my studies to try and figure out what to do next. I ran to my cards, the I Ching, astrology, and began to ask a thousand questions. I stayed up all night, asking in every way, shape and form, all with the same theme.

"Why?"

Eventually, the answers made themselves clear.

"This is just the beginning. There is more on the horizon. Be open. Be ready to go."

Looking back, I realize I was opening myself up for the adventure as a whole, opening up my personal vessel for The Voice that would eventually visit and for all the events to follow.

I stayed up all night making notes, writing as much as I could. As dawn broke, I knew I had to get these notes to Fellini, if for nothing else than to say I had tried. I felt an ethereal connection and I couldn't see the harm in sharing what I had gathered. I was also extremely fatigued and not necessarily thinking clearly. I felt like I was being led there. I had come so far, I felt I at least owed it to myself to listen.

I didn't know which hotel Fellini was staying at. Usually celebrities don't leave their real name at the front desk, but I had to give it a try. I was determined and thought I would just call every luxury hotel in L.A. to find him and let fate play itself out. I also had the sense they were going on a trip soon so I had to act fast. The first hotel I called was the Hilton, which was right next door to the restaurant we had eaten at and by some miracle or some other form of intervention, it happened to be where he was staying.

I was now convinced more than ever that I was meant to share my message.

I threw on a jogging suit, hopped in my car and sped off to the hotel. Not wanting to invade his privacy too much. I was aware that I was probably already overstepping my bounds. All I wanted and needed to do was to drop off all the pages of notes I had written and stuffed into a vanilla envelope. My thought was that maybe he could find use for these notes and the spiritual messages directed towards him. I would leave it at that.

It was seven in the morning and I stood quietly holding my package in the back of the line at the front desk of the Hilton; there were several people ahead of me waiting to speak with the concierge. I was very tired and unkempt, and I didn't pay attention to who else was in line. I just stared down at the ground, numb and confused at what all was transpiring so quickly. Then, all of a sudden, the man standing in front of me in line turned around, grabbed my shoulders and shook me intensely. It was Federico!

He pulled me aside and we sat together. It looked like he hadn't slept at all either.

"Did The Voice tell you to come here? Do you know what they want?"

I repeated once again that I didn't know which voices he meant, but that I was drawn to do several inquiries into the mystics after our meeting.

Fellini barely glanced at my notes. He said he had received another call from The Voice when he got back to his hotel room the night before. He was told that he must wait down by the front desk at 7 a.m. to find "The Spiritual One" to accompany him on a trip he was taking.

I then told Fellini that part of my personal prophecy from Geri is that I would hear Voices from somewhere not of this world.

"Come with me to my room, I have much to tell you," he said with great enthusiasm. "We have a trip to go on!"

When I walked into his room, I found Andrea and Maurizio already there waiting. They were not happy to see me. In fact, Andrea told Fellini in front of me that he believed this was all a trick and that I was in on it. I was very uncomfortable, but Fellini just ignored him, exclaiming that he was happy to have found the female muse that The Voice claimed he needed.

Fellini sat me down and explained everything to me—his vision, his meeting Castaneda, his quest for Don Juan, the trip, the film, and of course, The Voice.

"You are to be part of this group. You are to be a muse, the spiritual one that will help us. This work will be important."

I still didn't understand, but I immediately accepted my role. This felt true. It was a higher purpose. I didn't know where it would lead me and I was a little scared, but finally, all of it—my legacy with spirituality and other realms, my career path, my desire to be something more, my move to L.A.—it all made sense.

The phone rang. Fellini just stared at it for a second. He feared who or what was on the other end. He picked up the receiver in one quick motion, as if he knew that if he paused he might not ever get the will to answer. After a quick and curt hello, Fellini's face dropped. He staggered, nearly dropping the receiver. It was as if he was aging in front of my eyes. He didn't speak. He just listened. That's simply what you did when The Voice called.

"You have found the spiritual one. Take care and wait for our next instructions."

Fellini slowly relayed the message along with our new names, or rather designations that were given to him by The Voice. He would now be The Green One. Andrea would be The Blue One, Maurizio the Yellow One, Sybil The White One, and I was to be The Pink One.

"Well, pink is a very loving color," I said, laughing nervously. Later on, others in Fellini's circle would also get color designations either directly from The Voice or through Fellini. Tullio would become The Violet One. There would be another of his contemporaries that would be The White One, an Orange One, and a Grey One.

The Voice didn't explain the reason for the colors, and we briefly tried to figure it out. But we were interrupted by Sybil coming into the room.

Once she was caught up to speed, you could see the jealousy in her eyes. In her mind, she was supposed to be the Spiritual One. She made this new arrangement, my new place in the group, very difficult. Since the travel plans had already been set and paid for, there was no room for me, and nobody was going to go out of their way to try and fit me in. Fellini pleaded to find a way to include me, but he was alone.

"Don't you understand? This is so clear!"

Nobody wanted to hear. They felt they had their group set and I was the outsider. Not even Fellini could convince them. I was on my own.

I accepted that my part in this adventure would come later and simply wished them well on their journey to Tulum. In fact, I took them to the airport. As they departed, Fellini looked unsettled. He knew this wasn't right and he worried about the potential repercussions. I wished him safe travels and went back to my apartment, completely exhausted.

As soon as I got there, the phone rang.

I answered, and in that instant, before anyone even spoke, I began to shake uncontrollably. Sweat poured down my face and the air felt thick, as if I was choking. It would feel this way every time "You" called. I heard what sounded like the crackle of a walkie-talkie, an unusual static that was muffled, as if it was coming from far away.

Then, The Voice spoke.

"We are with you. We are one with you. We have always been with you. We are watching. You are The Pink One as you have been told. You must stay close to The Green One. You are now part of a very important mission. You will see messages in music, light, and colors. You will learn and understand. We will show you. We will help you. This is now your life's work. Go! You are closer than you know. Go!"

Then the line disconnected and I just stood there in a full body sweat, in terrified awe of what had just happened. Up until this point, I don't know what I had truly thought of Fellini's tale. There were parts that made absolute sense to me, signs and coincidences that were just too obvious to ignore. I believed Fellini when he talked of The Voice, even though I was unclear what he meant. I even believed right away that it was probably not of this dimension. If my studies had taught me anything, it was to be open to the unknown, to be aware enough that we human beings are only conscious of a fraction of what is really out there. Still, I knew he was a man of great visions and I wasn't completely positive of what was true and what was his translation of a vision. In short, even though I knew I was involved in something unusual and grand, I wasn't exactly sure what it was or what I believed. The phone call left no doubt. This was happening, it was real, and I was now an integral part of it.

Early the next morning, I packed, loaded up my car, and started the journey to Tulum. This team had a head start in their adventure, but I would catch up. I would play my part. I would make sure we followed The Voice's plan.

It seemed critical to me that we do so.

Chapter 7

A Journey Off the Path

There is this gap in the story, the two days I wasn't with the entourage as they traveled together on Castaneda's very own personal scavenger hunt. Again, the idea, from a practical filmmaking standpoint, was to show Fellini some of the beautiful and mysterious locales of the northern part of Mexico, ending with the center of the spiritual haven itself…Tulum. Beyond that, Castaneda wanted Fellini and his followers to engage in a spiritual quest of sorts to both connect him to the eccentric writer and to prepare him for his attempt at tackling the complex works of Don Juan.

These two days are a bit of a mystery. They were a mystery even back then. As I wasn't there, I have only the party's recollections and written accounts to go from. What little information I did get out of them was confusing and difficult to understand as they were trying to process exactly what they were experiencing, and really, why they were even here taking part in this seemingly asinine experiment in the first place. Even for a director as eccentric as Fellini, this pre-production process was out of the ordinary and no one but the director himself was excited about it. Everyone was looking to him and he was very dismissive of them, focusing on the path in front of him, hoping to find the magic he sought.

I am hesitant to even write about these two days, but it's a necessary bridge in our story, especially because The Voice was becoming more of a presence to the group in that time, setting the stage for my upcoming reunion with them.

TOWARDS THE MOON WITH FELLINI

Federico, Andrea, Maurizio, and Sybil set out to explore this elusive, magical circuit that Castaneda had provided for them on a convoluted secret map. These were all locations that were incredibly difficult to find but all places that corresponded to Castaneda's tales. The group, specifically Fellini, was told that after visiting these places, he would have a deeper understanding of the teachings of Don Juan, that he would be ready to not just offer the story, but also be shown a higher purpose. Fellini craved this more than anything. He was a suspicious but willing player.

Castaneda's methods in just about everything he did would be debated over the years almost as much as the validity of the man himself. Throughout the course of his life, he had his avid followers who were basically cult-like and his critics who were just as strong in their convictions that Castaneda was nothing more than an esoteric fraud. He was an extremely intelligent man who, as his popularity grew, emphasized the need to maintain his mysterious reputation, especially when it came to those he could influence with his supposed abilities and intellect. He was a notorious quick study of the people he interacted with, allowing time for preparation before any meeting. He had a knack for adjusting to any scenario and presenting himself the way that would benefit him most, often bordering on manipulation. When it came to something so deeply personal as spirituality and our need as a race of beings to seek something greater, there were many he faced that were open to anything and everything he had to say.

Fellini was one of them. In fact, in a 1988 interview, Fellini had this to say about his initial feelings on Castaneda:

"I was fascinated by the overall idea: that of a scientific man, an anthropologist, who starts with a speculative, scientific purpose, a man who keeps his feet on the ground, watches where he's going and literally looks at the ground, in fields, in vegetable gardens, in glades, toward the hills—where mushrooms grow. This man of science then finds himself, after initiation, following a path that brings him into contact with some ancient Toltecs. I like the route supplied by a scientific, rational curiosity, a route that he took with a rational attention and which, at the same time, led him toward the mysterious world, a world we define in a vague way as irrational."

But there was something unusual and apparently untrustworthy about Castaneda and this road trip he had set them on. To others in the group, it felt like it was almost designed to trick Fellini into becoming more of a believer. Others would later validate that fear. In an interview, a director by the name of Tony Karam (*Casa Tibet*) said he was at one time very close to Castaneda until he began to feel that his stories and methods of sharing these stories were both fake and potentially harmful. He said in the interview that Castaneda had an uncanny ability to capture the psychology of a person and tell them whatever they needed to hear. Even more interesting, he recollected how Castaneda had told him how excited he was about the prospect of Fellini doing a film on his teachings and about his sending Fellini's entourage out into the jungle. Castaneda allegedly admitted to him that building up the mystery was part of the process and he intended to show Fellini some "magic" along this route the group would take. It was all designed to further build upon the Castaneda legacy and to get Fellini committed to the project.

The group progressed through their skepticism with hope and the understanding that as far as they and their path was concerned, the Puppet Master was running the show.

Over the next two days, the group hopped from destination to destination. They'd find themselves in these remote corners of northern Mexico and at each location, they would find a message left for them, supposedly by Don Juan or some other shaman mystic, that would lead them to another location. They would also be told how to explore these places. ("You must feel the air on your face as you drive.") According to a later interview with Andrea, they arrived at Chichen Itza, the legendary city built by the Mayan civilization, and were told that it was the negative pole of the world. They were then told to join the *positive* in Tulum.

The trip was filled with these types of cryptic messages. The group grew even more skeptical and as the map jumped from location to location, that skepticism jumped to frustration and even anger. They felt they were on a wild goose chase that was never going to amount to anything. Every place they visited, they were promised to see something magical, a bit of proof to Castaneda's tall tales, but they would leave with nothing but another message. For a while, Fellini remained steadfast, convinced they were on the right path and that Don Juan held the answers he so desired. Infighting began between Andrea and Maurizio over Sybil's affections and everyone's need for Fellini's attention. At the start of the mission, the group was already beginning to dissolve, finding themselves driving around in a virtual vortex while they sought the path to enlightenment.

Complicating matters further, I was told that The Voice got in touch with them a couple more times while they were on their adventure and each time the message was the same.

"You are heading in the wrong direction. This is not the path. Be careful. We are watching you and watching out for you. But be careful. This is dangerous. But we are assisting you as best as we can."

This further frustrated them, especially Fellini who was too stubborn to simply give up this quest for Castaneda's truth. The Voice, this voice from the moon, was already terrifying Fellini and he began to realize that he was ignoring it. He wondered what the repercussions might be if he failed to listen. Nevertheless, he marched onward, always hopeful. The group marched along with him, ending their scavenger hunt in Tulum.

They were tired, frustrated, irritable, and unsure what was going to happen next.

Chapter 8

I SEE YOU

As the rest of The Colors took their trip to Tulum, I made my own. I knew that there would be a challenge, not just in finding them but also convincing them of what I knew, what I heard and the role I believed I was supposed to play. I was the outsider after all and yet another person competing for Fellini's sought after attention. In their eyes, I had already diverted this trip enough and I'm sure they, with the exception of Fellini himself, were glad to be rid of me.

The drive down there through the harsh Mexican desert, seedy towns, and dense jungle would be the least of my concerns. However, I was now on a higher mission and nothing would stop me from playing my part in this grand plan.

Hearing from The Voice had absolutely terrified me and thrilled me at the same time. I knew I was on the verge of taking a giant step into that great unknown. All that had been predicted had thus far come true. I had moved to L.A. on a very specific premonition and it had played out. There was no way this was a coincidence. Geri had told me that the planets and the stars would open for me. I had no idea she had meant literally.

I knew that I was now part of something not of this world, and this was no longer my adventure to let go. The Voice had chosen me to be a part of it, first by lining me up to be in the right place at the right time and then by calling me directly. You had reached out with a distinct purpose. I was told that it had taken a lot of energy for them to do so and that they couldn't and wouldn't be ignored.

This group was to be a channel for them, whoever they were. This group, *our* group was important. They also knew that not everyone in the group believed. At least not yet. Fellini was floating alone in seeking this cosmic wave and, yet, even he was on the wrong path. I needed to be there with this group, to be part of the knowing that would come our way, a conductor of the energy that would be needed to form this connection.

I was simply following the plan that was being placed before me. You had demonstrated their power to me, whoever or whatever they were, and I had no reason to do anything but listen and obey, to trust in something greater. In terms of my role in this grand scheme, it was their words and not mine. Who was I to ignore them? These were the thoughts flooding my mind as I drove for two days down to Tulum.

I had been there once before, where I had collected the slideshow photos that triggered Fellini's first reaction in my apartment. I remembered Tulum's unsettling beauty. It is a truly vibrant place, with stark colors and a tapestry of a godlike coloring kit. Everything about the area seems rich and full. There are constant sounds of living beings big and small…and perhaps those that aren't living. It is a haunting place, especially when you start thinking back to the ancient civilizations that once lived there and the rituals they performed for years in that area. For as beautiful as Tulum and all of the Yucatan is, it is also filled with death.

In my previous trip, I had gone with a tourist group and had lucked out in that upon arrival, almost everyone else in the group got sick except for me. Many had to stay in the hotel as we visited some of the temples and other ritual sites that are sprinkled throughout the land, remnants of a very old and mystical civilization as mysterious as any in the history of mankind. That meant less people around than normal and more opportunities to explore and truly experience the environment. Beyond taking photo after photo, I truly allowed myself to *be* in the place, to experience what I could there and to connect to the energy that filled the area. I had mixed feelings of awe and of horror as I thought of what was done for the sake of the gods that ruled the minds of men at the time. Yet, I felt like I was standing in a place that was once run by people who were connected to something greater, that something that I have spent my life seeking and I couldn't deny the excitement I felt because of it. I allowed myself to wander and explore, waiting for signs, letting the universe know I was open and willing to receive.

A few years later, the universe had answered and here I was driving through the pale, dusty desert, the cartoonish Joshua trees and endless telephone poles on my way to a more beautiful place, to this greater adventure. I found it sweetly ironic that I would first have to drive through miles of nothing to get to possibly the meaning of everything.

The desert and its vast, empty wastelands makes you go slightly insane mile by mile. But it also opens you up to all possibilities. There are little to no distractions. It is literally just you and your thoughts and if you give in, you can be awoken to answers to some of your most fundamental and challenging questions.

Of course, sometimes the mind can use a little push.

Toward the end of my first day of driving, I pulled over in the desert and took a rather high-powered hallucinogen. Now I reveal this in the interest of honesty. I was not a major drug user, though I did smoke my fair share of marijuana, which was not unusual for my generation. Still, I rarely tinkered with anything harder, and when I did, it was less for recreation and simply to open up my mind. Again, I was hesitant about even including this in the book as I don't want anyone's opinion of my tale to come down to the simple assumption of "Well, she took drugs." That would be a disgraceful simplification of everything that happened and, well, it just wouldn't be true. Almost everything that I experienced in my time with Fellini, every phone call and direct contact with You happened during moments of one hundred percent sobriety and clarity. It would only be when I was seeking answers on my own that I would allow myself to open my mind to external influences.

To be honest, I don't even remember what it was that I took, but I remember that it hit me right away. I suddenly felt both very alone and very in tune with my environment. I saw that I was both in and on my way to a truly magical place. I looked up to the heavens and gasped as I saw what I believed to be the legendary Akashic records, the manifestation of the astral plane in all its glory. I saw those planes of existence, energy, and what appeared to be universal coding open up and encircle me. I could see back millions of years to when the sand was under water, when particles formed the bottom of what would eventually become the foundation of this desert. I saw the Earth as it was pounded by meteors and asteroids and other cosmic matter. I saw how the Earth had shaped and formed right here. Yes, this was a grand place, an important place. This was a place to communicate, to channel, to listen.

This was a place to connect.

That night, I pulled my car over to the side of the road and tried to sleep. I was only asleep for what felt like a matter of seconds before I became enveloped in a strange vision. Even in my dream state, I wasn't sure how this was happening. My hallucination had worn off hours prior and now I was simply tired, giving into the crash that comes after the high. Yet, here I was in the midst of a crystal clear vision.

You was here too.

This solo journey down to Tulum would be the first time I would get a clear look at what I assumed was the face behind The Voice. It was a quick, fleeting glimpse, but one I would never forget. It would have been easy for me to write this off to the drug I had used earlier in the day, but the image itself was too clear. It wasn't a dream. I was involved, physically present in the midst of something else. This would be the first of four times over the course of my adult life that I would see You and each time, it felt different than any other dream. That made me believe.

There were four of them and they were towering over me, looking down. Even though I could see they had bodies, the shapes constantly shifted so there were no details I could make out. They were in some type of dark, smoky colored robe, but again, the vision of their bodies kept going in and out. Their faces, if that's what they were, are hard to describe. Think of how it looks when you see an oil spill either in your driveway or in a pool of water when the light hits it. It is constantly swirling, a rainbow of colors that never stops moving, blending together, pulling apart. Their faces were made of changing colors. I thought I could make out black eyes and even a small nose, but I couldn't be sure. As real as the vision was, they were a blur. I had the sense they appeared to me that way for a reason, as if showing me too much right now would send me over the edge. They weren't wrong. I felt complete terror. As such, there was only a simple message I heard in the vision, the only words spoken, not out loud, but in my head.

"Don't be afraid. We're here to assist you."

Then I awoke in a full panic, sweating, short of breath, all energy drained from my body, just like I felt during the phone calls. It would be some time, almost two years, before I saw You again and for that I would be grateful. It was too much. It was too much for me to handle by myself and I believed! I needed to get to the group. I began to understand that we could only handle this as a unit, a collective force of energy that would support each other and work together to open up the right lines of communication. This was too much for anyone to do alone.

The second day, I drove as fast as I could, crossing the desert and entering the thick jungles of Tulum, not knowing how I would find them, what would happen when we met again, or where we were going. All I knew was that something big was happening here and we needed to be together to fully experience it.

Chapter 9

The Trip to Tulum

After receiving the call from The Voice and then experiencing my vision, I began to understand more clearly Fellini's obsession with Castaneda. He too was looking for answers, some way he could wrap his mind around what he was experiencing and explain it. That's a very human impulse, this need to understand before we can accept. For as much as he lived in and wanted to be engulfed in the supernatural, Fellini had to know what it all meant.

Despite the warning messages he was receiving from The Voice, the always stubborn Fellini was convinced that Castaneda could provide some answers. Either he was going to be the one directly involved with The Voice or he would be able to give some insight into the nature of The Voice and why it was reaching out to him. Fellini hadn't really had the opportunity to discuss The Voice with Carlos in L.A., and truthfully, The Voice wasn't as much of a presence until after that meeting. Fellini thought that following the plan and meeting Castaneda in the jungles of Tulum would be the ideal setting to finally get some answers.

I pulled into Tulum and as soon I got there, I was instantly reminded of its beauty and its thick cloud of mystery that seems to settle and never break in that mystical place. This is a land of the ancients. There are beliefs the locals share that these ancients were highly evolved and possibly from another planet, sent here to advance mankind. There are thoughts that global and possibly interstellar events have taken place here, including one that split the continents and shaped our world. To this day, there are strange phenomena that occur regularly, including unusual sightings and feelings and… voices. There is a power you feel when you pull into Tulum, despite the throngs of tourists that flock there every day to see the preserved structures. All the commercialism in the world can't dilute the history of what happened here and how that history has forever impacted the aura of the place.

I parked my car and quickly realized I had no idea where to go. I asked around for some names of hotels. Since Tulum itself is a beach town, there are men who make their living offering boat rides to tourists. As soon as I got there, I was swarmed by short men with sun-drenched faces and smiles, aggressively trying to get me in their boat, constantly hustling with their broken English. Not knowing where else to go and thinking this might help me clear my head, I hopped in one to take a quick tour.

A very short time later, we rounded a corner of the beach and I saw one of the area's most popular hotels, one Fellini referred to as the Tower of Babel. It was grand for this area and I was marveling so much at it that I almost missed who was walking on the beach in front of the hotel.

"Federico!" I yelled out and Fellini lifted his head in surprise. He couldn't tell from this far away who I was or how a stranger would know him down there. Nor could any of his entourage who were following close behind. I told the boat man to take me to shore. It was unbelievable to me that I would run into Fellini and the group mere minutes after my arrival.

As I hopped off the rickety craft, I noticed right away how exhausted everyone looked. I could tell that the first couple days had not treated them well. I could also sense that Sybil, Andrea, and Maurizio were not happy in the slightest to see me. Andrea and Maurizio instantly started talking to each other in Italian while Sybil simply glared at me. This was what I expected, but it still made me feel unsettled and very unwelcome. They weren't my primary focus though. I greeted Fellini with a big hug and the ramblings of an excited child, letting him know why I was down there, that I had received a call from The Voice and a vision and how I wanted to help.

Fellini lit up like a Christmas tree.

Despite or maybe because of the energy of the group, I was the breath of fresh air Fellini wanted and needed. I would be with him as he had his final meeting, a defining one in Fellini's eyes with Carlos. After spending a couple days trying to get a feel of the environment, following Castaneda's path and hitting wall after wall in their search for something special in the Yucatan, Fellini was ready to discover more, discover *something*. He still had the film on his mind and was excited about the possibility of bringing Don Juan's tale to the public in a new light, but now he felt more pressing matters, things that he couldn't shake…The Voice.

The group was set to meet Castaneda at the hotel that afternoon. We wandered the beach until the meeting. While I knew they weren't happy to see me there, what with their frustrations of the last couple days also piling up, I couldn't believe just how harsh they were right in front of me. All three of them had their doubts about The Voice and the validity of not just Fellini's communication but also of Carlos and his potential involvement in this whole thing. The last few days did little in making them believers. Seeing me down here, knowing that I was encouraging Fellini to pursue this magic and that I was now talking of visions and voices of my own, they became convinced that I was working with Castaneda in a sort of con, that I was one of his *women*. They made me feel alone. They made me feel foolish. They made me feel disconnected from a group that I felt The Voice wanted me to guide.

"We don't know this woman. We don't know what she wants," Maurizio pleaded to Fellini. "It doesn't make sense that she should just show up like this down here."

They even tried to use warnings from The Voice to convince him.

"Perhaps this is what you're being told to watch out for," Andrea said. "Perhaps she's involved in the danger."

The more it went on, the more defiant I got. I was here for more important reasons than their acceptance. I didn't owe them or anyone an explanation. I had been pulled into this by bigger forces and I had a job to do. Lucky for me, Fellini listened, but chose to ignore them…at least for the time being. He said he felt comforted by my presence and that ended the discussion. Besides, he was about to meet Castaneda again and this time he was going to get the answers he sought.

That meeting lasted five minutes.

Five disappointing minutes for all of us.

Castaneda arrived with his own entourage in tow. Castaneda's people, more specifically his three women, were unusual and even a little frightening on their own. All of his followers around the world were devoted, absolutely cult-like in their obsession. Yet, unlike most other cults, they had a reputation for not so much linking themselves to the man, but rather his ideas and the mysticism of the shamans as a whole. As such, they viewed Castaneda as merely the vessel for these messages. They honored and respected him, but the word was they tolerated some of his eccentricities only because he had been chosen. We would have much more intimate dealings with his followers in later years, but during this meeting they were there just to let their presence be known, to show us that Castaneda was more than just a man, he was a carrier. They hung in the background, quietly waiting and watching.

Carlos himself was unimpressive. I myself had been a devoted follower of his words since I was twelve. I truly thought of him as a spiritual leader, a living being in tune with something more. I too wanted to be in the *tonal* and with the *nagual,* two of his primary teachings. His writing had influenced and impacted my outlook on the world and all that we can and can't see. My dealings with Fellini aside, I also was attracted to the idea of coming to Tulum for the possibility of meeting a man I greatly admired. We all think these people we put on a pedestal will have something powerful about their presence.

I would quickly learn that not everybody is the Dalai Lama.

Carlos was a short, paunchy, unshaven, plain-looking Latino man in a ragged Hawaiian shirt. He had a warm enough smile, but a posture that looked wary and almost weak. He looked like he carried a burden on his shoulders, but he also looked like a man willing to play the martyr, a man who wants you to believe he is something more than he truly is, something great. In reality, he was simply average.

"My friend," he said, coming in to give Fellini a hug. Like Castaneda's companions, we in Fellini's group just hung in the background, watching the meeting of these two brilliant minds and seeing what would unfold. Before Carlos could get a word in about the project or the journey the group had taken over the past couple days, Fellini cut to the chase.

"Are you the one behind these voices?"

Carlos backed up away from Fellini with a puzzled look on his face. Castaneda was a man that didn't like surprises, a man that was always in control of any and every situation.

"Voices?" he asked confused and smiling nervously.

Fellini proceeded to explain the calls he had received in both Rome and L.A. and how they had impacted him and set him on this quest.

"Are you making these calls? Is Don Juan behind The Voice?

Carlos' reaction to this is what I remember most. He looked stunned. It was just a fleeting look on his face, but I remember this as the moment I started to doubt the power of Castaneda.

"What calls? What voices? What are you talking about?" Castaneda was losing control of this conversation and he was getting angry. "As I told you before, I was told that I would meet you, but that's it. I have no idea what you are talking about."

He had never met anyone as stubborn as Fellini, who insisted that Carlos was somehow pulling the strings. Again, Fellini needed something to help him make sense of this all and he had focused so much on Castaneda giving him the answers. To come this far and not get anything was unacceptable, especially after the frustrations of the past couple days.

Castaneda got scared. We all saw it. He didn't understand what was happening and you could see it in him. He was sweating, his eyes were wide and his entire posture changed. It was the moment this project, this collaboration between the two, truly fell apart. This was beyond Carlos, way more than he bargained for, and it freaked him out.

Again, he shook his head and said to Fellini, "I have no idea what you're talking about."

"You must know," Fellini insisted. "You must."

With that, Castaneda lost his composure. He began to rant about the "fools" who were out to persecute him. He talked of the CIA and other organizations who were trying to capture him and the dangers of his life. He wondered if we were being followed or if we had led "them" to him. As quickly as he arrived, he said a quick goodbye and left. He folded into his flock of followers and disappeared. None of us would ever see him again.

Everyone was disappointed. Andrea and Sybil began to realize this trip and all their running around was for nothing. Maurizio started to realize that there would be no movie and he started thinking of all the money already wasted on this supposed "pre-production" trip. I lost faith in a guru of sorts that I looked up to and admired. And Fellini realized he was not one step closer to getting any of the answers he sought.

Plus, The Voice was silent. Both before and right after the meeting, we hadn't heard anything on that day from The Voice. Here we were, at a place where we thought its presence would be the strongest and instead, You had abandoned us.

We collected ourselves in the hotel room as best as we could. If tensions were high before, they were at an extreme level now. This was a disaster and everybody was looking for someone to blame. Nobody wanted to talk, so it simply boiled underneath, waiting to explode.

Fellini would eventually come to terms with the disappointment in Carlos and the abandoned project. In later interviews, he would

TRIP
TO
TULUM

Drawing by Federico Fellini for the graphic novel, *Trip to Tulum: To the real Helen, Christina "enigmatic and luminous" friend with enthusiasm and happiness.*
Federico, Roma 1991

VIAGGIO A TULUM

Drawing by Federico Fellini for the graphic novel, *Trip to Tulum*:
*To the beautiful Cristina, Helen with gratitude and wishing you with much
enthusiasm for being almost always so close. Good Luck.*

Federico, Roma 1991

say that he was still confused about Castaneda and whether or not the self-proclaimed shaman even really wanted him to make a film. He would look at that portion of the trip to Tulum as a wild goose chase of sorts. He would also at times wonder if Castaneda's followers, who were very guarded of him and his secrets, somehow influenced the writer to not help with the movie.

"My film project based on Castaneda's stories upset, alarmed, or alerted a particular group of people," Fellini said in an interview with an Italian newspaper years later. "Castaneda must have belonged to a well-organized group with an ideology that its members believed in fanatically, which also has underground informants scattered throughout the world. I am convinced that Castaneda was, in a certain way, under the power of this mystical group. The 'friends' of his books tolerated Castaneda, but when they realized that a film would disclose their mysteries, they intervened to scare Castaneda."

That is a possibility. Personally, I believe he was scared and couldn't handle what Fellini was telling him about The Voice.

Right after the meeting happened, Fellini was still very upset. He had not only lost a project that he thought could pull him from the doldrums of his stagnant career, he was also no closer in understanding the origins of The Voice and what You wanted from him and why.

The plan was to head back to L.A. to regroup and figure out what to do next. They would fly and I would have to get back to my car and drive. We were all disappointed, but I still had hope. I believed there was something else on the horizon. I knew more was coming and that we hadn't heard the last of The Voice. Everything was happening and Tulum was just a distraction, a deviation from the path…or maybe it was exactly what we needed to infuse each other into our lives.

Either way, I knew this adventure was just beginning.

Chapter 10

CHE DIAVOLO CI FACCIAMO QUI?

Federico wanted to drive home with me. He was exhausted, frustrated, and confused. One of the last things I heard him say before we all left Tulum revealed exactly where he was at mentally and emotionally.

"Che diavolo ci facciamo qui?" he said to no one in particular. "What the hell are we doing here?" He was speaking to the ethos, to the universe, to The Voice.

Part of his exhaustion came from the group. Maurizio and Sybil were not good with each other. Maurizio had an interest in Sybil, but she had shown some affection for Andrea and Fellini. This twisted love triangle had made its presence felt during the entire trip and combined with the frustrations of the trip itself, had created an unhealthy environment with some unwanted tension. As for Andrea, without a story, he began to get bored with Tulum, Fellini, and this adventure as a whole.

Fellini tried to tell the others that he was going to drive with me, but none of them would let him out of their sight. They were very vocal about how little they trusted me and there was no way they were going to leave Fellini alone with someone they considered a crazy, obsessed stalker who may or may not be playing games with Fellini.

They flew back to L.A. and Fellini would tell me later that his confusion put him in a major depression. When the great director had an idea, it consumed him. He could think of nothing else and he needed to see it through. This particular project came to no resolution and he didn't know where to go or what to do next. He felt The Voice had guided him this far. Even if he misunderstood part of what You was trying to tell him, he found it confusing that The Voice had simply abandoned him, especially now when he was so lost. On the flight home, he wondered if he had angered The Voice and this bothered him for other reasons altogether.

For the longest time, he had held onto a touch of skepticism. There was always a part of him that entertained the notion that this was all an elaborate plot or hoax, perhaps orchestrated by Castaneda himself. However, the final polarizing meeting between the two convinced him that Castaneda had no part, which meant The Voice was something truly extraordinary. He wondered if he had perhaps missed his opportunity by not listening completely and focusing on the wrong direction. This possible opportunity missed ate at Federico on the way back and he hoped and pleaded to the ethos to send The Voice his way once again, despite his ever-growing fear of it.

As soon as he got back to the hotel in L.A., he received a call.

"You have been on the wrong path. You did not listen to our warnings. You have been pursuing the wrong man. Castaneda has nothing to do with this. You must get back on the right path. All of you. We are here to guide you."

Then You told him about colors and music.

***

I had a long drive home and too much time to think. In just a short amount of time, I felt beaten, yet hopeful. The brief trip down was so exciting for me as I felt enlightened and eager to let the others know that we were on the brink of something spectacular. But once I saw the group dynamic and their alienation of me, it was a blow. Still, I had started to play my role. What came out of that trip was the shedding of our egos or at least the first attempts to lay the groundwork for humility to this higher power that was trying to reach us. I honestly believed that.

Still, it all felt so unsatisfying in the moment. Only later would I discover that we were really there to drop all of our last false images and illusions as to what we were dealing with and whether or not we should be in this together. This trip would close the door on Castaneda and open us up to other possibilities. But there was such a long way to go for us to connect and work as a group to receive You's message… especially since only Fellini and I heard and seemed to care.

It was on the way back that I would start to form my own theories on the true nature of You, though I knew it was premature. I was now firmly convinced that they were not of this world, nor of this dimension. They displayed too much in terms of knowledge, power, and control to make me think anything else. I knew they could get in our heads. They could tell exactly what we were thinking. They usually showed up via telephone when we needed them most. Other times, they let us alone in our discovery. They showed they had the ability to physically impact our world though we would see a lot more of that later. They showed us true, pure magic. They also showed us that they knew something important and that they were trying to figure out how to share that knowledge with us. This was a potential block for us and even for them. The process of communication was a little confusing and I felt like You was trying to work it out themselves how best to share with us. I was convinced it had to do with the transfer of energy and that the only way we were going to be able to receive it was as a group.

Despite their feelings about me, I decided that if I met with Fellini's entourage again, I would become the glue that held that group together. That was my mission. I was now giving myself over to the will of The Voice.

As soon as I arrived back in L.A., I was called by Fellini and told to come meet them at his hotel. He was told specifically by The Voice that I was now a part of this. Needless to say, this infuriated everyone else. They were simply following Fellini's orders and his apparent contact with this mystery figure. They hoped that would end now that Castaneda was out of the picture. Remember, Maurizio was here trying to get a movie done and Andrea was trying to find one to write. They didn't have time for me. Fellini was steadfast and told them my involvement was now crucial.

Not only did he need me, The Voice commanded it, and Fellini was now going to listen fully and completely to The Voice.

"Christina, you need to be here," Federico said pleadingly, but also with a renewed sense of enthusiasm. "I have heard from The Voice and they told me that I need the Spiritual One, or The Pink One as you are now called. You must come immediately."

I was thrilled. They needed me, or at least Fellini did. Not long after I got off the phone with him, I received another call. Before I even answered, I knew it would be The Voice.

"You must go be with The Green One. He needs you. They all need you. Go. You must stay with The Green One. You must sleep with The Green One. We are with you."

I must *sleep* with The Green One? I was to sleep with Federico Fellini? Of all the requests or messages we had received from The Voice, this was the most intimate and some would say invasive yet. It was emotionless in its request, or rather command, as well. This is something we would agree on as we kept getting calls. We didn't think You had any concept of real emotion, at least human emotion. Everything was very robotic, even down to the sound of The Voice! There was never any joy, anger, pride, frustration, etc. There were just commands, endless commands.

I have to be honest. I was more than willing to comply with this one.

I craved Fellini. I was so incredibly attracted to him, not just because of who he was and his good looks, but also because of how connected I felt to him in this adventure. I absolutely wanted to have sex with him and if it meant furthering our adventure with The Voice, all the better.

When I got to the hotel, I again walked into a hostile environment. I didn't care. I would work on building those relationships piece by piece as I could. I knew everything started with Fellini and he would have my attention, especially tonight. I explained what I had been told from The Voice and before anybody could protest, Fellini said he had been told the same thing.

Nobody knew what to say. It wouldn't be the last time.

That evening, Fellini and I crawled into bed together and I can't even begin to describe the excitement we both felt. From the moment we met, we knew we had a special connection. We were the only true believers. We were there for each other. We were where the bond began. This made sense to both of us. As soon as we got under the covers, the phone rang.

"You are not to have sex. You are there simply to hold each other, to sleep with each other. That is all."

Frustration doesn't even begin to describe what we felt. This was pure torture. After how difficult the past few days had been, we both felt ready to experience something magical with each other. We both wanted each other and we couldn't understand why they wouldn't let us. We would figure out later that it was probably to keep the innocence of our relationship, especially for the many times we had to convince his wife and my future husband of the true nature of our pairing. We both knew that the only way we were going to learn whatever it was The Voice was going to show us was to follow its orders.

Plus, we were both scared of The Voice as well and didn't dare refuse it.

So we simply laid there, cuddled up in each other's arms, forming a different kind of connection, a closeness that would last for the rest of Fellini's life. It was that night, in that bedroom that we established our own unique relationship with each other. While we would always have sexual chemistry with each other, we never once ever acted on it. I would be a lot of things to Fellini; his muse, his confidant, his friend, his psychic. I would never be his lover. That was not part of the plan. To this day, I still wish and wonder what it would have been like if we had consummated our relationship, but then I am grateful for the relationship we did have. It led to many memories, to many adventures and to an understanding partnership that was just for the two of us. I wouldn't have traded that for anything. And it all started that night as we rested in each other's arms, contemplating the meaning of all of this.

Unfortunately, The Voice had other plans for that evening.

At around 4 a.m., You called again.

"The Pink One must go to The Blue One. He is sleeping. You must bring him back to the group."

This didn't surprise me. I had thought about this on the way back from Tulum. I wasn't exactly sure why but, as I mentioned, I believed my role was to keep everyone together and that You would call on me to do so.

"You will have sex with him."

What?!

I wasn't expecting that. I didn't want that. I didn't know if I could. I instantly felt awful inside, cold and shaky. I believed we all had to do whatever The Voice told us, but this was trying to convince somebody who had shown me nothing but contempt that he had to have sex with me. Andrea was a very good-looking man, but I didn't want this. I wanted Fellini.

As I hung up, Fellini could tell I was upset.

"What's wrong, Christina?" he asked and I told him.

Needless to say, he was livid. He didn't want to let me go. He told me not to and I wanted to do nothing but listen to him, to crawl back into his arms and lay by him. I wanted to protect him and have him protect me. I didn't even want to see The Blue One.

Yet, something in my mind, perhaps even You, made me feel like I truly had no choice. Like it or not, we were now in this and there was no turning back.

"I have to listen to what they say," I told Federico. "I have to do what they ask. There are more important things here."

After much protest, Fellini relented and let me go, also wondering where The Voice was going to draw the line or if it would be up to us at some point. This was a great test for both of us.

And for Andrea.

"What do you want?" The Blue One asked when I knocked on his hotel room door. I had to remind myself that it was 4 a.m. after all and

I was the last person he wanted to see during the day more or less in the middle of the night.

"Uh…we just heard from The Voice" I said timidly, trying to muster my courage.

"Yeah," he said and you could hear the tone of disbelief and annoyance in his voice.

"The Voice said I'm supposed to sleep with you."

When Andrea realized what I meant, he was stunned. He couldn't believe that I would even try to be with him. He couldn't believe Fellini would let me go. He couldn't understand who this "Voice" was and why it was commanding people to have sex with each other now. I tried to explain that I was also confused, but that I believed we had to listen. I tried to explain that there was something bigger going on here. It was not an easy conversation.

Andrea and I were both very attractive people. Truthfully, I did find him very physically appealing with his jet black hair, slim figure and deep Italian tan. And I was a model, after all, so I hoped he had, at the very least, a physical attraction to me as well. After some back and forth, I convinced him to let me in.

It was the strangest love-making we both had ever had. It was awkward and uncomfortable for both of us. I was doing this out of an obligation to The Voice. Andrea was doing it so as not to make waves. He was very uncomfortable because he thought we were being watched. He still didn't believe any of this. If Fellini and I were a ten on the spirituality chart, Andrea was a one, maybe a two. This was too much for him and now he was just going along for the crazy ride. Neither of us was very happy with this particular stop.

When we were done, Andrea's phone rang and I answered. It was The Voice telling me that I had done my part and that I was to return to Fellini, which I did. Federico was clearly distraught but didn't ask me any questions. He just clutched me close to him and we laid there, both bewildered and terrified, wondering what the hell we were involved in.

The next day would get even weirder.

Chapter 11

A Symphony of Colors

If my "interaction" with The Blue One the night before had any positive result, it was that it brought me closer to The Green One.

Literally.

The next morning, as we all sat having breakfast, Fellini would not leave my side. He held me close to him, clinging on to me like an infant, not that I minded. He did this in front of everyone, almost as if he was letting them know that no matter what they thought I was now here to stay and that he and I had our own special connection.

Andrea and I were understandably awkward with each other and the leers toward me and tension between everyone else continued. Suddenly, Fellini broke the constant arguing with an announcement that he had received another special message from You…perhaps the strangest yet.

"We are all going out today to buy musical instruments and tonight, at midnight, we will make music."

There was just silence.

I can't remember if it was Maurizio or Andrea, but one of them was the first to speak, telling Fellini what we were all thinking individually.

"I don't know how to play any instruments."

We all nodded in agreement, perhaps the first thing this collection of misfits had in common with each other. As with all things, Fellini was not swayed. For him, it was simple. The Voice had told him we would play music together at this particular time. We would do so and trust that something would happen.

"But why?" someone asked. "Why would people who can't play music have to play music? What is supposed to happen?"

Fellini explained that The Voice had begun to talk to him about colors and music and how they might relate to what You was trying to reveal to us. He still had no answers but he was convinced enough to take this next step.

While I was intrigued by the concept of the power of colors and music, a subject I would study much more in depth over the next few years, I had a different theory. I didn't think the activity itself mattered. I thought The Voice was trying to bring us together. It was trying to get us to have an exchange of energy, a connection that we would all focus on. It was meant to show that this constantly arguing flock of egos could all sit at the same table and take part in something together.

I tried to explain my theory but of course, I was brushed aside, fully ignored by all except Fellini who just looked at me and nodded. It made sense to him as well. Nobody else believed but they all went along with it. After all, anything was better than sitting here arguing all day long.

And just maybe we could have some fun with it.

We all ventured first to a local Robinsons-May store to buy outfits. Once the decision was made by all of us, or rather *for* all of us by Fellini, we decided to go all out and make it a production. We were going to get instruments, but first we were going to get outfits that matched our personalities and our colors.

While the men picked out suits or other pieces of clothing that matched their colors, the girls picked out fancy dresses and blouses, all competing to look better than each other. Even though I was The Pink One, I was focused on my role as the unifier and I chose a multi-colored dress that incorporated everyone's color. I was trying to build the harmony and I thought Fellini's little musical adventure could actually help us. Even though everyone continued to treat me poorly, I decided to be calm, patient, and understanding. I would help facilitate this group to whatever it was You wanted. I was all in.

Next, we visited an independent instrument shop in L.A.'s Larchmont district. Keep in mind that it was the Eighties. As such, Fellini got a synthesizer that he was immediately intrigued by. Andrea enthusiastically grabbed a guitar while Maurizio reluctantly bought a saxophone. Sybil, not wanting to be outdone by anyone, bought the most expensive synthesizer in the store, one that would probably be too complex for most experienced musicians. I got a Les Paul electric guitar, bright white, in the shape of a lightning bolt. It was called the Explorer, which I found fitting. Our "band" was almost complete.

But we had one more member who needed to join...my roommate Brinke. I had kept her up to speed on everything that was happening with Fellini and the group. She knew all about the trip to Tulum, The Voice, and its unusual requests. She was in awe and that morning, before we went on our shopping spree, she told me that she had gotten a call from The Voice saying she should join us. She was to be called The Violet One.

Needless to say, we were all skeptical, especially Andrea, Maurizio, and Sybil. Now here was my roommate. This just furthered their distrust of me and my intentions. Even Fellini and I had our doubts. It seemed highly unlikely and unusual, but who were we to say no? Nothing You had done had really made sense up to this point, so who were we to judge or question? She would prove to be a breath of fresh air for this group, a new energy added to the mix. Brinke's presence made everyone relax just a little bit and shift their focus off of the feelings we had for each other. Brinke would be our band's bass player.

That night, close to midnight, we sat in Fellini's suite, dressed in our new clothes, with our instruments set up as best we could. We all looked around at each other not knowing what to expect, but thinking this was maybe just a little bit ridiculous. But there was also a bit of hope in all of us (even the others would later admit) that something magical might happen here. Maybe we would all collectively see the power of The Voice at work. Maybe we would learn a little about the power of music and how it affects things beyond our cognitive capacity. We were being guided after all. Maybe it didn't matter that none of us knew how to play. Maybe we would just play and something beautiful would happen. I know I hoped. I was excited.

The clock struck midnight and we all picked up or switched on our instruments. On Fellini's cue, we all began to play our symphony, our celestial rock song, our audible call out to others in our universe and the next. We began to play the song that would change the world.

We were terrible.

Honestly, dying cats sounded better. It was the loud, screeching noise of a group of wailing infants banging on pots and pans. It was exactly what you'd expect from a group of people who didn't know how to play music. It was awful. There was no magic here.

We all looked at each other and shook our heads in disbelief. What did we expect to happen? Why would we think that we could just play? It was ridiculous. Only Fellini wouldn't accept the inevitable, that this had been another confusing task by The Voice. He kept insisting that we try again, waiting for the miraculous to occur. Just like the conductor in his film *Orchestra Rehearsal,* he was losing control of his musicians. We could see the determination in his face. He was trying so hard to make something of beauty come out of his synthesizer and he was maybe the worst of all. Finally, as we clamored away, we all started smiling. Then we were giggling and finally laughing at the absurdity of it all. Eventually, even Fellini joined in. We all sat there, a group of musically challenged artists, rolling at how stupid we all looked and sounded. Eventually a hotel security guard came to stop us because of noise complaints from other guests and mercifully, the concert was over.

I will always remember looking over at Maurizio, who was just shaking his head, wondering what the hell he had just paid for!

Once again, we just couldn't understand the point? What was happening here? I took some comfort in the fact that for a brief moment, we were all laughing together, connecting. I truly believed that was the point, but even I thought there could have been another way to get us there. Still, a connection of any kind was progress for The Colors.

It didn't last.

The phone rang and Fellini answered. He was given two simple messages. As for the music, The Voice said that we had done enough for tonight, which I thought was an understatement! The Voice also confirmed that Brinke was now part of us, the color Violet, and that she was to sleep with the Yellow One…Maurizio.

This would prove to be the unraveling of our group. It was inevitable. The frustration, confusion, jealousy, expense and so on were just getting to be too much to bear. Human beings need answers and we weren't getting any. All we got were vague messages and seemingly pointless tasks to do. Though she had basically ignored Maurizio, Sybil wasn't happy that he and Brinke were now supposed to spend time together. It brought up all the bad feelings between this twisted love triangle once again. It didn't help that Maurizio, who still felt something was going on between Andrea and Sybil, was attracted to Brinke and willingly went along with The Voice's request. Sybil stormed off and the rest of us went to bed, perplexed yet again by the path You was putting us on.

The next morning Sybil came back to tell us to our faces that we were all sick, that we were involved in some sort of devil worship, and that she was done. That would be the end of her involvement and quite honestly, we were all okay with that. She had been a constant source of negativity and we all now thought that Brinke, who was enthusiastic, open and light, was brought in to replace her.

Still, we were all in a funk. We didn't get much sleep. Maurizio was beginning to realize that he had to stop spending his father's money on this trip as nothing was going to come out of it. Andrea wanted to get back to his other projects. Fellini was starting to feel like this was going to be a constant manipulation of his time and energy with no answers. He feared The Voice, but he was now getting angered by it and the lack of results. Meanwhile, I was worried that we had continually missed our opportunities to learn more, to see more because we couldn't get our collective shit together as a group. We were all supposed to share this experience and bring it in together and it just wasn't happening. I also wondered if we were continually misinterpreting what The Voice was trying to tell us or if we were taking things *too* literally. I too began to wonder why these evolved beings, as we thought they were, couldn't be clearer with us, why we were being directed so poorly.

Mainly I felt that we had failed them. We hadn't been open to the truth. Here we were, a collection of artists, talented people, some of whom were actively seeking cosmic philosophies and secrets, and we couldn't or wouldn't take in what You was trying to teach us. Maybe they gave us more credit than we deserved. Maybe we weren't the ones they should be trying to communicate with, to bestow wisdom upon.

Maybe we weren't special. Fellini was starting to think the same thing. He was done.

"It's time to go home."

Chapter 12

You Must Go to Him Now

We had spent these days together on an adventure of a lifetime, chasing an elusive author, traveling to places of deep, dark magic, connecting physically and spiritually, allowing fate to guide us, letting something we couldn't understand pull the strings of our lives. We did it all in the hopes that we would be shown something greater, that we would be allowed to learn the universal secret. We did it all to evolve.

As I watched Fellini head into the airport, I realized that we had nothing but an interesting story. That was it. We were nowhere closer to learning any hidden secret about what else is out there, on this plane or the next, then when we started. That realization hit me like a ton of bricks.

Little did I know that our meeting and our experience were really just setting the stage for the truly supernatural to occur. It was the appetizer, a gentle way to ease us into some of the truly dangerous and thrilling things we were about to experience over the next few years, both alone and together. It was the preamble to a lifetime of study and discovery for me, the initial push to guide me to learning more about what's out there, and my place in the grand scheme of things. That trip planted the question that I have been chasing an answer to ever since.

Why?

At the time, I only felt disappointment and sadness. I had hoped for so much more. I had upended my life to come be a part of this and I was given every sign that something momentous would occur.

On the surface, I tried to play if off. Most people, after all, would have been more than content to share that adventure with someone the likes of Federico Fellini. He was a great artist and this was a surreal and thrilling few days. And hey, I got a great dress, an expensive guitar and a great tale to share out of it. Deep down, though, I was hurting. The quest for answers aside, I was afraid that this would be the last I would ever see of Fellini. In our short time together, we had been joined by a belief, a yearning, and a literal calling. We were two people who really understood each other at our very core and those partners don't come along very often. I felt we were meant to do so much more with each other and he felt the same. I even was going to miss the rest of the group in the sense of what could have been. I felt like we had been pulled together for a very specific reason and we had failed as a unit. I knew that was something that was going to haunt me.

Federico and I hugged each other with every ounce of strength in our bodies. A few words were exchanged and just like that, he was gone.

I went back home to try and process all that had happened and before I even had a chance to breathe, the tears started flowing... and the phone rang.

"You can't let him go. You must follow him."

Over the next couple months, that would be the recurring theme of the phone calls I would receive from The Voice. Fellini would tell me that he was getting similar calls telling him it was important for us to stay near each other. I think the only reason we didn't instantly get back into each other's lives is that we needed time to recover from those few days in Tulum and L.A. and to process what was happening. The Voice, however, didn't have the patience and You started to make its presence felt in an almost frightening way.

Upon their return to Italy, Fellini tried to distract himself with a project, once again getting back to work on his film *Ginger & Fred*. He would tell me in phone calls and letters that he was still perplexed and frustrated by all that had happened. He was, after all, on a quest to make a masterpiece of spirituality and he was beginning to come to the realization that it was now never going to happen. For someone who liked to think of himself as a channel, that was difficult to accept. He wondered if there still wasn't work left for us to do together. He wrote me the following in a letter less than a month after he left L.A.

"I think of you often, dear friend, and after all that has happened it is the least I can do. I'm still a bit shaken and confused, and of all this extraordinary and mysterious experience, your image is the most concrete, the most relaxing, the most solar. I'd like to have a long talk with you about this someday."

Fellini tried to see what, if anything, could be created by this experience. Despite his frustrations and the strange tension, Andrea also reflected on the experience and realized there was something here that could maybe be shared, if we could all wrap our heads around the experience. Andrea and Fellini briefly contemplated the idea of a script for making a film anyway, but it never felt right. Andrea would eventually turn our adventure into a fictionalized work that would polarize him from the group. Before that happened, I received this letter from him, a much kinder message that truly surprised me. Time apart to reflect can have a significant impact on a relationship and perhaps even offer some perspective.

"I'm sure Federico and Maurizio have told you all about the recent developments in our incredible and fascinating story…we have all been in touch with You and everything is becoming more magical and real at the same time."

The fact that Maurizio and Andrea were now having direct contact, as well as Fellini and myself, gave me a spark of hope that maybe our work wasn't done yet. Through these letters, they would not only give me updates as to what they were doing, they would also fill me on You's presence in their lives. Over the next month or so, The Voice would bring new members into the group, including Tullio Pinelli, who for some reason was also called The Violet One and a musician, who's name escapes me after all these years. He would be known as The Orange One, though he was never as involved as

Rome, Nov 6, 84

Dear Christina,
            I received your poems and the photos,
and I wished to thank you for this affectionate 'hel
lo' you sent me.

                        I think of you often, dear friend,
and after all that has happened it is the least I
can do.I'm still a bit shaken and confused, and of
all this extraordinary and mysterious experience,
your image is the most concrete, the most relaxing,
the most solar. I'd like to have a long talk with
you about this someday.

                        Will you come to Rome as you'd men-
tioned? And have you had any news from Sophie? I've
begun again my work on the preparation of my new film,
which should start in January, but I really hope I'll
be seeing you before then.

                        I'll stop my letter here, because if
I should let myself go I'd fill sheet after sheet .
Do write to me whenever you can and feel like it. I
send you a big, warm hug, dear Christina, and I wish
you all the very best. Sincerely,

the rest of us. There would then be a Gray One and another White One, as well as a few others, all helping Fellini as he continued to get calls himself.

While I was thrilled to hear from them, it was also incredibly frustrating. I felt like I needed to be there, that I should be experiencing this all with them. I became completely detached from my life in L.A., only taking comfort in the few times I would receive a phone call myself.

And truthfully, those phone calls were becoming more and more invasive.

"You must stop crying."

"You must go to him now."

"We are going to help you."

"You must make the sacrifice."

"You must go to him now."

"We no longer want you to eat meat."

"You cannot use any kind of drug."

"You must go to him now."

What started as a voice potentially guiding me to a deeper cosmic understanding was now starting to tell me how to live my life. The Voice also started to manifest itself more and more physically, making things disappear, shifting objects, and so on. If I was hysterical and not listening, You would render me unconscious. I began to see just how powerful You was and it terrified me. The Voice became less guiding and more demanding and I started to wish, at times, for it to leave me alone.

Instead, You was trying everything to bring Fellini and I back together. We would have mysterious connections. For example, one time he fell down the stairs of his house and twisted his ankle. He picked up the phone to call an ambulance and there I was on the other end. The Voice had told me that Fellini needed me. For my birthday, I held a fancy party in New York with family and friends. I hadn't told Fellini about the party. Out of the blue, Fellini called the hotel I was staying at and said The Voice wanted us to talk. More and more, The Voice guided us to each other and more and more, we began to feel that we should listen…both out of curiosity, fear, and a sense of responsibility.

Our work wasn't done. Our relationship wasn't done. In one of the last letters I received from Fellini after this adventure, he wrote the following:

"The fact is that what I should tell you, and I want to tell you, requires some calm, some meditation, and the possibility to recall things if not clearly, at least in harmony with the most private, most secret and unknown parts of myself."

He needed me and I needed him. Together, we realized that we needed to learn more. We needed to heed The Voice once again and accept that our fate was intertwined and that our adventure was just beginning.

The next stop was Rome…and I was going.

Chapter 13

UNDERSTANDING THE COLORS

Why colors?

As I sat alone in Los Angeles, missing my friend, hearing about his continuing adventures and hoping and praying for an eventual reunion, I had a lot of time to contemplate. I had space to assess what had happened to all of us. I went to my cards, my stones, my own inner voices, all that I had trusted for so long, seeking meaning and clarity.

As my mind filled with questions, one kept repeating itself over and over again, one I couldn't shake.

Why was it so important for You to give us color designations?

I knew enough to know that nothing the Voice did was trivial. Even if we couldn't understand its purpose, there *was* a purpose. Everything You did had a reason. Unfortunately, they simply weren't good (or we were ill-equipped) at communication. It was up to all of us—well, at least Fellini and I—to figure it out. The Colors seemed incredibly important, but why? Also, why were certain people in this adventure given colors while others weren't? Why these *particular* colors?

Just to recap, here is what we were called:

- Fellini—The Green One
- Maurizio—The Yellow One
- Andrea—The Blue One
- Sybil and later Philipo (a tarot reader Fellini had met)—The White One

- The Musician (whose name escapes me after all these years)—The Orange One
- Tullio and Brinke—The Violet One
- A mystery man (who I never met)—The Grey One
- Me—The Pink One

Some of these came to be during the trip and others upon Fellini's return to Italy. What these people had in common is that they were all in some way instrumental in Fellini's life at that place and time. It seemed undeniable that Fellini was the main target of The Voice, its channel to communicate to humanity. With his history, it made sense. We were all there to help him reach his potential as this vessel. We were a part of his life, we were a part of this experience, and we each had a role to play.

The color green is often associated with power as well as growth and understanding. It is also the heart chakra. Yellow goes with intellect and varying levels of responsibility and strength. Blue is loyalty, scrutiny, trust. Orange is confidence and support. White is innocence but also coolness. Violet is mystery, ambition, royalty. Of course, they all have their negative connotations as well. We saw more than glimpses of the dark sides of The Colors on the trip and the adventures to follow.

Pink, my color, is love, romance, friendship, nurturing, encouragement. More than anything, pink is *unity*. It is a blending of colors. To me, this specific color designation and the emphasis You made to Fellini to find me, to find The Pink One, made me feel like I was supposed to bind us all together. Whether successful or not, that was my mission…and it would continue well after Tulum.

I believe that using colors was the only way You could truly communicate with us. It was the only way they could let us know not only our importance, but also that we were dealing with something beyond our understanding. I constantly reminded myself that we were targeted by beings not of this planet, or at least this plane of reality. After all that had happened up to this point, I could no longer deny that fact. Even back then, I was ready to accept that these were higher powers. They were different. They were alien. Exactly who or what, I wasn't sure, but I knew enough to know they were not us. As such, they couldn't communicate like us. Sure, they could synthesize a human voice and appear on the other end of a phone call, but when it came to communication, to real communication, there was blockage. There had to be, or they would have simply been clearer in not only their instructions to us, but also the purpose and meaning behind what we were doing. They could talk to us, but they couldn't *communicate*, not really.

Or maybe it was on purpose. Maybe they wanted us to look deeper, to open ourselves up to something greater and take on the challenge of exploring. Maybe they wanted to bring us closer to them and this was their way. Maybe they didn't want to just give us the answers, but rather they wanted to simply help us find them. Unfortunately, as our constant doubt and squabbling proved, we were far from ready. Still, they tried and I believe they tried through the use of colors.

As I mentioned, they didn't seem to understand human emotion. They were procedural in their demands, business-like in their communication. To me, honestly, they seemed evolved beyond emotions but also aware that we still had feelings in our DNA. We *feel* and those feelings and emotions often guide us and propel us in our adventures, especially as we seek answers to the universe's greatest questions and mysteries.

So how does a "race" of highly evolved, emotionless beings identify with and communicate an important mission with a walking, talking cluster of emotions and questions?

Color is a universal constant, much like sound. Color is a bridge between intellect and emotion. Color is a bridge between us and them. Color is energy and these were energy beings. Color is emotion and we are emotional beings. Color could be the tool to help us evolve together and find a middle ground. In that middle ground was where we would uncover and understand their message.

If we could just get there.

Rome, Jan 12, 85

Dear Christine,

         this isn't the letter which I planned to
write, and which I would have sent you if I hadn't been
so busy with the film I'm working on.

         The fact is that what I should tell you,
and that I want to tell you, requires some calm, some
meditation, and the possibility to recall things if not
clearly, at least in harmony with the most private, most
secret and unknown part of myself.

         Anyway, I'm writing to thank you for your
affectionate letter, so much like that of a good, protective little sister, and for the altar-like card with the
cake for my birthday.

         I think of you often, and I'll call you one
of these days. I hug you with great affection,

As I sat alone in L.A., I was just beginning the process of forming these theories. Again, my conclusions would take years and countless other adventures to take shape, and even today, I'm only slightly confident in these beliefs. It's just so far beyond anything I ever expected to experience.

It wasn't just the colors. There was also the musical instrument experiment, one The Voice closely linked to our colors. Before our sad band played its midnight rock opera, The Voice made sure to emphasize our colors and in that, I felt like we missed something. Our colors were supposed to link up with our sounds, an individual harmony within the greater sound we were creating together. It's sad to think of now, but for us, it was just a bizarre request, one we had fun with and didn't take too seriously. Now, after years of researching, analysis, and self-reflection, I think something completely different was maybe supposed to happen that night.

Sound is another universal constant. I think You was trying another way to reach us and make us understand. Especially because sound and color are so closely linked. There is a theory called *bio-geometry* that studies the power of colors and assigns musical notes to go along with them. Using both together as a creative energy source is supposed to help a person tap into multiple energy fields. When that happens, we open up our human consciousness and allow for growth and understanding to occur. As color and sound are universal resources, the two working in harmony are very powerful and help us reach beyond what our human conscience can understand. They not only help us see further, they also help us dig deeper within, unlocking components that are otherwise inaccessible. When these are unlocked, we connect to the greater mysteries. We find answers. We find God.

We evolve.

You gave us color designations and introduced us to the power of sound and colors as a way to let us know what they wanted. They thought we were more evolved than we were. We proved them wrong.

But there was still a chance.

As I started to develop these theories, it became even more critical for me to be with The Green One, to be with all of them really. We had missed the opportunity in Tulum and L.A. That was obvious. Yet, You was still in contact. There was still a chance we could get this right. I still didn't know what the purpose was, and I knew I was just scratching the surface, but if we could all just get together again and be open to the experience, who knew what we could find?

First, I had to get to Italy.

Chapter 14

YOU ARE ONE OF US

Yes, it was time to get to Rome, but how?

For that, I first turned to Geri. After all, this had all happened because of her premonition. She had set the wheels in motion, even telling me that at one point that I would be moving to Rome! She had literally created an entire chapter of my life, perhaps the most important, and during a brief trip to New York just a month or two after my Tulum adventures with Fellini, I once again looked to her for guidance.

"See, I told you," she said, not wavering for one second when I explained to her all that had happened.

As a colleague of hers, I extended her the professional respect to not ask how she was able to see what had happened, though I was and have always remained extremely curious.

"Now they are telling me that I'm supposed to move to Italy to be with The Green One…to be with Fellini," I said.

"Of course, I told you as much," she responded.

"But why?"

"That I don't know, but why does it matter?" she asked, seemingly irritated with my questioning. "You want to be with him, yes?"

"Yes, I feel like we're supposed to be together helping each other. I feel like that's what You wants us to do. Only together can we figure this out."

"Then, that's all there is," she replied, trying to end the conversation.

"Who are they?" I asked and she paused, staring at me for quite some time.

"I don't know," she finally said.

"Will I ever find out?"

"I don't know."

We sat there for a few silent moments.

"How am I supposed to get to him?"

"I don't know, Christina," she said. "But I know that you will."

Finding my way to Rome was going to be difficult. I had spent a lot of my savings on the move to Los Angeles. While I was starting to book a few acting and modeling gigs in L.A. and developing my psychic reading business going, I was still very short on cash, especially for something like international travel. Even back then, flights to Europe were not cheap, not to mention lodging and spending money. The idea of moving there was even more daunting. The whole situation was incredibly frustrating.

What made it tougher was that I kept hearing from the group that *was* over there and how they were trying to work together to figure out what had happened. They were interested now. Fellini told me in a correspondence that The Voice essentially hinted that he was supposed to make a movie about our adventures, a project that would help You spread its message to humanity. He wasn't a hundred percent certain of this message, but he felt confident enough and was exploring the possibility even as he resumed work on his film *Ginger and Fred*. Though he wouldn't get into too many details over the phone or in the letters he sent, he too acknowledged that our work wasn't done. The trip had to be about more than what we had experienced. We both agreed that the fact The Voice was still trying to communicate with us showed that we were still involved.

"Help me!" I would yell to the skies, waiting for The Voice to answer. "If you want me to be there, help me!"

While Fellini contemplated a project that he believed might change the world, the others were looking to resolve their involvement in this mystical adventure, some guided by their own time to reflect, some by personal (and possibly even selfish) motivations, and some directed by The Voice itself, or at least so they said. The Blue One, Andrea, said he finally heard from The Voice. I never really talked to him about it in great detail so I don't know if it's true, but he was very convincing and explained an experience like we felt when we received phone calls. Plus, correspondence showed he had softened up to me, almost inviting me to be a part of his life as if nothing bad had happened between us. Whereas he once tried repeatedly to have me expelled from the group, he now considered me a fellow adventurer. He told me he was trying to convince Fellini to let him write a screenplay based on the experience. The two had several talks, and plans were made to at least explore the possibility. That was about as committal as Fellini would be.

Maurizio and his father were also still somewhat involved. Then there were others joining, including The Grey One, the other White One (Philipo), Tullio and The Orange One, the musician sent to the group to help them possibly understand the musical connection. In a letter to me, Andrea describes The Orange One's involvement; how You brought him to the group.

"Everything is becoming more magical and real...(The Orange One) is very nice and it didn't take him long to get into the spirit and meaning of all this. Federico gave him his keyboard, as he was told, and the keyboard woke him up in the middle of the night playing an amazing cosmic wave which kept him frozen in awe for a long time."

There was more The Voice wanted of us and the group was experiencing it. Meanwhile, I was stuck across the world, getting nothing but invasive messages about getting to Italy and changing my lifestyle.

I was lost. Here I was living and working in Hollywood, meeting A-list celebrities, going to exclusive parties, finding a life that millions dream of, and I was disconnected from it all. I was on the cusp of once again finding myself in the limelight, in that tight inner circle that can make or break you as an artist and a celebrity and I wasn't even present. My heart, soul, and mind were in Italy.

"This isn't fair," I cried out. "What am I supposed to do? You want me to be with him, to go to him, but I can't! Help me. Tell me how."

This was a common conversation I would have in the late hours of the night, screaming to the heavens, to whoever was listening, feeling like I was screaming to myself. On most nights, I would scream myself to sleep. Occasionally, You would answer with a simple phone call and a simple message.

"Stop crying."

But there was one night where the response was different. I tried to understand why You chose this particular night to reveal a little more to me. It was after the New Year, 1985, I was back in L.A. fighting the urge to give all this up. I knew in my heart that I wouldn't, but my frustration at being stuck while everyone else seemed like they were moving was reaching its peak. I still felt like I was an important piece of this puzzle and yet, I was the one who always had to make the extra effort, the one who hit roadblock after roadblock on this journey. It was getting to be too much and I was beginning to feel it taking its toll on me. Perhaps that was why I received this special phone call.

If The Pink One, the binding force in this group, quit, then there would be no chance for the message to be fully received, understood and presented. At least, that's what I thought at the time.

They told me to go to him. They told me it was important. They told me to find a way. That was my responsibility, but on this night, as I reached a mental breakdown, they revealed something more…

"You must stop crying."

"I'm sorry," I said, fighting the fatigue that came with each of You's calls. I had apologized every time they told me to stop crying. It had become habit.

"You must go to The Green One."

Every time they gave me this command, I would instantly follow up with a question they wouldn't answer:

"How? "

Tonight, I asked something different, something telling of my current state.

"Why?" I asked weakly and You responded with silence. And then something opened up inside of me. "Why are you doing this? Why are these things happening? Why must I go to him? What does this all mean? What is the point?"

With that, they hung up. I didn't stop. I kept yelling my questions, releasing all my frustration, letting it pour out, perhaps seeking a place that I could either accept or move on. Yes, this was good. This was catharsis. Maybe this would help me let go.

The phone rang again and I answered.

"Hello."

"You are permitted to ask us one question."

I froze. You had never ever given me, or as far as I knew, any of us that option. They gave commands, not answers. I had a million questions. Picking one on the spot was next to impossible, so I went with the first thing that popped into my head.

"Who are you? Are you reincarnated? Is there reincarnation? Why—"

I would have kept asking questions until I lost my voice, but You cut me off.

"There are many lifetimes. There are many beings. They all experience many lifetimes. You have been here for thousands of years. You are one of us. You always will be one of us. You will see. You are special. You are The Pink One."

With that, they hung up.

"Holy shit, what the fuck did that all mean?!" I said out loud, this time to nobody in particular. Not only was I stunned to have gotten a response, I was now tasked with trying to figure out exactly what You's reply meant. First things first, they essentially confirmed the idea of reincarnation for me. I had to let that soak in for a second. I know I will have skeptics in reading this book and I seriously don't blame any of them. I mean, this was one of THE biggest questions, especially in my studies of the various faiths and beliefs of the world. You had just literally filled me in on a universal secret, even if it was in their own vague, non-

FEDERICO FELLINI

Rome, July 15, 85

Dear Christine,

I received the letter in which you tell me
that you plan to come on July 27th. I'll see you with great
pleasure, even though I must tell you that my work will keep
me busy from morning till night, because we have promised to
finish the film by the end of September, and therefore the
time is very little. Anyhow, it will be wonderful seeing you.

Of Maurizio and Andrea I have had no more news
concerning the project you know, and when I see you I will
tell you something else which disappointed me and puzzled me
about the Yellow and the Blue. There are also more news of
which I'll inform you when we see each other.

I'm tired, listless, and I think your enthusiasm will do me good. Stay well, dear Christine, I hug you
with great affection, simpatia and curiosity,

descriptive way. Still, my attention was more focused on the other part of their answer.

"You are one of us. You always will be one of us."

Seriously, what did that mean?! Are they us? Are we them? Or... am I them? If so, then who am I?!

I didn't bother asking again because I knew I wouldn't hear back. I was now on my own to figure out what You meant. If this new information did anything (besides blow my mind), it reinvigorated my commitment to You's mission. It was now more important than ever that I get to Italy. I needed Fellini's help just as much as he needed mine.

Over the next few months, I would receive more phone calls and they would get more and more disturbing in nature. The Voice began to tell me things about Fellini, things that he had never shared with anyone. After keeping them to myself for a long time, I finally opened up to Fellini about these messages and they scared him. There were phone calls between us that ended with him and I both in tears. I was learning things about The Green One that got at his very core. Out of my complete love and respect for this great man, I can't share them here. There is a part of me that yearns to, that believes full disclosure will help me find some of the answers I still seek, but I just can't. My relationship with Federico simply means too much, even this many years later.

I believe You was sharing these private secrets for a few reasons. First, they were still offering proof of their existence and power. Second, after opening up to me, I believe they now trusted me more and were willing to share more. Finally, and perhaps most important, they were using this to push us together. It had now been months since our adventures in Tulum and I still wasn't in Italy. The time was now. They let me know in yet another phone call.

"You must go to him now. There is no more time. You must be with The Green One."

Instead of just asking the simple question of "How," I asked in more detail.

"How I am to get there? I can't afford it. I don't have the money. How am I supposed to pay for a flight that costs $1,200? How?"

You hung up. Not long after, my doorbell rang. I opened the door to see nobody there. I looked up and down the hall and saw nobody coming or going. In fact, the hall was empty except for a shoebox on the ground right outside my door.

In it, was $1,200 in cash.

I took the box inside, set it down on the table and counted the cash. I was calm. By this point, I was no longer surprised.

I would never be surprised again.

Chapter 15

Reconnecting in Rome

"I'm tired, listless, and I think your enthusiasm will do me good."

I received those words in a letter just a couple weeks before I went to Italy. Since discovering a box of cash outside my door, a gift and a very clear sign of the next step in part of this adventure, Fellini and I had been corresponding about a good time to visit. Of course there was some urgency on my part. I felt I had already been delayed too long and The Voice was now relentless in its demands for me to get to see him. I suppose that since they removed the last obstacle, they could see no reason I wasn't there already.

But I knew il Maestro, and with him, everything had to be handled somewhat delicately, especially when it came to his schedule. Even as we connected in our phone calls and letters, I did sense a conflict in him. While he continued to try and understand The Voice and its mission and his part in the grand plan, he also seemed at times to be distancing himself from the entire experience. Over the years, one thing I would learn about Fellini is that as much as he sought the supernatural, it did scare him and overwhelm him as well. While he craved to understand more about The Voice and why it was reaching out to our group, he was also getting slightly exhausted by all of it. I could sense that part of him wanted to leave the experience behind.

I was part of that experience. As such, there seemed to be some early hesitation on his part to have me come out to see him. He informed me how busy he was on *Ginger and Fred,* even as The Voice pressured him to take on this new project. I also knew that back in

Italy, he had not just his work but also his family responsibilities, affairs, and other commitments. L.A. and Tulum were an escape, a fantastical adventure, and I think at times he was truly on the fence about whether or not he wanted to continue exploring.

The Voice knew it as well. The phone calls increased in their frequency, to him and me. They also got more personal and that terrified him. More than that, for the first time, there seemed to be just the slightest hint of emotion in You's calls.

Frustration and possibly even anger.

After receiving pressure on my end, I convinced Federico that we were supposed to tell our story and that we had to do it together. He agreed that we should be together and with that, I was finally off to Italy.

In typical Christina fashion…I had no idea what I was going to do when I got there! I had no place to stay. I had very little spending or living money. I had no return ticket. I had no plans. I also had no idea what to expect, including from Fellini himself.

I realized how much in the past year my life had become about trips into the unknown.

Despite the long flight, I had dressed to the nines in a tight dress, a white, wide-brim hat, and dark sunglasses, wanting to make the best impression I could when I landed. Fellini had met me as a model, an actress, a beautiful woman, and that's what he would get when he saw me once again. Funny enough, when I stepped off the plane, I was instantly bombarded by Italian paparazzi snapping photos of me. I'm sure it was only because of how I dressed, and I got a slight chuckle when I thought how later, when they were developing their film, they would wonder who I was and why I was dressed like a movie star.

Fellini had Luca Verdone (the brother of the famous Italian comedian Carlo Verdone) pick me up from the airport. I could tell he immediately formed a crush on me.

"Fellini told me to watch out for you," he said and I caught the double meaning.

He took me to the Hotel Della Villa at the top of the famous Spanish Steps and just around the corner from where the great director lived. This is where my reunion with Fellini would take place. Excitement and anticipation can't even begin to describe how I felt.

"Christina!"

I heard that familiar voice of his call out my name across the lounge of the hotel and I instantly felt safe and comforted. In just hearing my name, I knew I had made the right decision and that now all would be well. Federico embraced me in a big hug and I could tell that part of him felt the same. We lingered there for a moment, two weary travelers once again brought back home to each other.

That first meeting was shorter than I would have liked. It was also overly crowded. Something I would soon learn, Fellini *never* traveled anywhere without an entourage. Along with Luca, there was also the renowned Italian journalist Vincenzo Mollica, a writer for the country's major newspaper Corriere Della Sera. Fellini had shared our adventures with him and he was excited to meet me and treated me very kindly. There was also Philipo, a brooding and mysterious young man who was enchanted by Fellini and who apparently also received a call and was our new White One. I got the sense he didn't trust me. Finally, there was the sweet and kind Fiammetta, Fellini's personal assistant and someone who would also become a very dear friend.

I had thought of this reunion for months and had visions of us re-connecting and suddenly discovering answers together, but it wasn't going to happen tonight. I realized just how much time had passed and how, in many ways, Fellini really had moved on with his life. He was known to do that. It was clear that our experience still weighed on him heavily and he was very pleased to see me, but I got the sense that he hadn't been obsessing about it the same way I had. I would soon learn in my time there, that wasn't necessarily true.

"Christina, I must get back to work for now, but we have much to talk about," he said.

"Yes we do, Federico. I look forward to it," and I embraced him in a strong hug once again.

"I am so happy to see you," he said and I could see the exhaustion in his face. He gave me one of his warming signature smiles and with that, he and his entourage were gone.

I stayed at the Hotel Della Villa for a short time and then Fellini introduced me to Contessa Grifeo, a wealthy aristocrat who owned several villas in Roma and set me up in one that sometimes housed celebrities, including Kathleen Turner and Francis Ford Coppola. Needless to say, I was overwhelmed. This was literally a far cry from my small apartment in Hollywood. I was finally here and I was extremely grateful.

As I checked in to my villa, I received a call from You.

"We are watching you."

That was it, but I didn't care. I had arrived in Italy, I was near The Green One and despite their involvement in getting me here and the bigger picture. I didn't have time for You right now. I thought I would get to their mission soon enough.

I spent my days seeing Italy, trying to learn Italian and visiting Fellini on set and watching him work. At the famous Italian studio Cine Citta Teatro 5, Fellini was king. He was constantly surrounded by people everywhere he went and he was worshipped as the leader of all Italian cinema. I watched as producers, assistant directors, actors, and other luminaries were hustled in and out of his offices. I was careful not to be too invasive, working around his schedule and soaking up my opportunities whenever they came. I had a beautiful place to call home and a thrilling tour guide in Federico, who introduced me to a host of Italy's elite, including famous domestic and foreign actors like Marcello Mastroianni, Sophia Loren, Giulietta Masina, Isabella Rossellini, Roberto Benigni, Ania Pieroni, Susan Sarandon, directors like David Lynch, famous authors like Gore Vidal and Leonard Bernstein, and respected politicians like former prime minister Bettino Craxi.

Everywhere we went, Fellini introduced me as his dear friend and his American psychic. He bragged about me and paraded me around with joy, showing everyone how much I amused him and how important I was to his life. I was his "little sister," which he called me with such kindness. He had me give him readings almost daily and we explored the esoterics together. We talked and talked, re-hashing all that had happened and our theories as to why and what to do now. It was bliss.

I stayed for a couple months, until my finances ran out; I had to get back to L.A. to make some money. It was a dream trip, a chance to spend some time with someone who was growing into more and more of a force in my life. It was everything I had hoped it would be, especially in terms of how it brought Fellini and I closer together on his home turf. It confirmed my belief (and Geri's prediction) that I was supposed to be over there. I don't know if we made any significant progress toward fulfilling You's mission for us, but it was at least a start.

Something else magical happened while I was there. I met the enigmatic Eugenio Cappuccio. I first met him at a lunch with Federico and some of his entourage. As we all chatted, Eugenio simply sat there and scowled at me. He was an assistant director of Fellini's, a very talented and intense young man who was extremely handsome. I could tell instantly that he didn't like me and he made me extremely uncomfortable. As we left the restaurant, Fellini's script supervisor Norma Giacchero, liking us both, paired me with Eugenio in the back seat of Fellini's classic white Mercedes. When I asked if he spoke English, he simply barked, "Yes!" I asked if he wanted to see a card trick and he simply said, "No" and remained silent for the rest of the ride back to the studio. Upon arriving, Fellini told Eugenio to show me around, which really irritated him. He didn't want to babysit this American girl. I found his attitude extremely annoying.

I told him as much. One thing I learned in my many travels to Italy is that the way to handle Italian men is to be forward and strong, to tell them what you're thinking and show them that you won't be intimidated by them. He confessed he thought I was only there to leech off of Fellini and I explained to Eugenio our true connection and that I was only there as a spiritual friend. After some back and forth,

The Meeting of the Colors. The Green One introduces the Pink One to the Colors. Sketch by Federico Fellini.

his disposition changed. He grew interested…and so did I. Later that night, as a way to apologize, he showed up at my door with flowers.

Over the next few weeks, Eugenio and I fell in love.

"You are not to see him. That is not why you are there. We are watching you."

That was all I received from The Voice and it was terribly upsetting. Once again, it was invading on my private life, dictating what I should and shouldn't do. As such, I was torn as to whether or not I should listen. What didn't help, was that when it came to Fellini and me and our mission, The Voice had suddenly gone silent. Unbelievably, inexplicably, frustratingly, after all the pestering, the nonstop harassment and commands to reunite, the moment we did, You went silent as to what to do next. Here we were, The Green One and The Pink One, along with the other colors, all back together in a place where we were now more open and ready to receive whatever message You wanted to send…and I got nothing but personally invasive phone calls into my budding love life.

Words can't begin to describe how frustrated I was at their conduct. I was perplexed and this was starting to get exhausting. It happened so much now that even trying to figure them out was too strenuous. I had spent some quality time with a soul mentor and I was content. If that's all there was to this trip, so be it. I was frustrated, but You's confusing mission was slowly sliding into second place in terms of my priorities. After all, I couldn't do what they weren't telling me to do. I was starting to tire of them. Truthfully, we all were. Still, You completely terrified me and I found myself backing away from Eugenio. I returned to America, wondering yet again what it was all for and if I had possibly missed something. I also now thought of my Italian love. Predictably, as soon as I got back to the States, I wanted to go right back to Italy.

But how?

Chapter 16

WHAT DID I DO?

By selling classic cars in the Grey Market.

In a weird twist of fate, earlier in the year, my BMW, the one I had received as a parting gift from my drug-dealing, good friend David, was stolen off the streets of L.A. It was quite a blow, not just because of how much I loved that car and it's worth, but also because, as anyone who has ever lived in L.A. knows, it's virtually impossible to survive in that city without a car!

So now I was not only lamenting and trying to find funding to get back to Italy, but I had to deal with the hassle of getting a new car. That's when David stepped in to help me do what he does best—find an angle.

"You should use the insurance money to buy a few cars in the Grey Market, get them over here from Germany where they're cheaper, and then take them out and sell them out in L.A."

David was a man of many business ventures. In one of those many ventures, he had a connection that led to a collection of BMW 3.0s in Germany. They were these beautiful two-door coupes built in the mid-sixties and early seventies as a way to get BMW in the "sporty driver" game. They were true classics, the style of the cars used in the hit show *The Man from U.N.C.L.E.* After making sure I wasn't going to be buying any stolen cars, I thought I'd give it a shot. I mean, I already had actress, model, psychic, and apparently lightning rod medium to aliens from other planes of existence on my resume… so why not the Grey Market?

The Grey Market doesn't really exist anymore, but back in the eighties, it was essentially a distribution loophole that allowed buyers in the U.S. to get products from overseas for less than the manufacturer intended. If you could find the right channels and the right buyers in the States, you could make quite a bit of money. Now it's more regulated, but back then, I could make some serious money on these cars.

That's how I found myself catching a cheap flight to New York to get to Port Elizabeth, New Jersey to pick up the first of several classic BMWs to drive back to L.A. Not surprising, with a little creative marketing and hitting up some contacts in my celebrity circles, I was able to instantly find buyers. I performed this little operation numerous times.

As soon as I got back from Italy, I knew I instantly needed to go back. So there I was back in New Jersey picking up another car and heading out west, this time with David along for the ride once again.

David was a great friend and an incredible confidant. With hours on the road to kill, I filled him on everything that had happened, from Geri's predictions to meeting Fellini, the trip to Tulum, the bond Fellini and I had formed, the crazy adventures, my trip to Italy, and so on. Of course, I told him about The Voice. David was a very spiritual man himself. He was also a devout reader of all things from Castaneda, so the details of the trip both fascinated and disappointed him. He really wanted to believe Castaneda or Don Juan was somehow involved. As for You, David shared my awe and wonder as well as my theories as to who or what they might be and why they were calling and interfering in our lives.

"They chose you," he would keep reminding me. "There has to be a reason for that. They chose you."

David, like many others I would include in my life and adventures in later years, helped me realize the significance of this event. I don't want to overstate the importance of my adventures as they're just one of many in this complex experience of our existence, but no important event should ever go ignored or neglected. Something extraordinary was happening here and I was a part of it. That had to be appreciated, revered. Mostly, though, it had to be followed.

"You need to see where this adventure takes you," David said. "You need to follow their instructions."

Without experiencing it himself, he would never know just how difficult that could be at times.

David stayed with Brinke and I for a few days in L.A., discussing all that happened and potential theories. I felt bad for him because he so wanted to be part of this adventure, to receive a call, a color, a job to do. He was more than open to it, he was essentially begging and pleading for the universe to include him in on its grand plan. Brinke too for that matter. After the phone call she received when Fellini was in town, Brinke never heard from You again. I think she was disappointed she didn't have a bigger part in the story. I remember sitting in the apartment sharing stories together and noticing both David and Brinke continually staring at the phone, willing it to ring.

You stayed silent.

Except for one moment, where David caught a glimpse of You in a rather unique and disturbing way.

Many of our talks together took place late at night over food, drinks and candlelight, hanging out in the living room. Many times, we would all simply crash on the couches, chairs and even the floor, too exhausted to even move ourselves to our respective bedrooms. After one such evening of living room camping in mid-October, almost a year after Fellini's visit to L.A. and our adventures to the Yucatan, I woke up to see a rather disturbed David staring at me.

"What's up?"

"Was it them?" he asked and I looked at him perplexed. "Were you talking to them last night?"

"What?" was all I could muster. I'm a very light sleeper and would know if I had gotten a call. I had slept through the night, I was sure of it. I certainly hadn't spoken to anyone on the phone.

And yet, I felt a chill go up my spine and something very faint pulling at the back of my brain.

"I tried to ask you last night, but you wouldn't respond," he said and I could see that while he was fascinated, he also looked ashen and a little shaken. "You just ignored me, even when you were looking right at me. You just ignored me and went back to sleep. It was like you were…"

"David, what are you talking about? I didn't talk to anyone last night." But I was beginning to realize that wasn't true. I could feel something different had happened.

"You were in a trance. You were here but you weren't…here."

I thought back to the tales of the man from the airport, the one who had brought Fellini the piece of fabric from his hat. He had shown up, fulfilled his purpose and once done, snapped out of it and found himself in total confusion as to where he was and why. The phone calls I had received had all been extremely powerful, draining, but I had never experienced anything like that. I had been an active player. Now, with David as my witness, I realize that I too could be rendered unconscious by You. I was truly at their will.

I had never felt so afraid of them.

"What did I do?"

"You didn't do anything. You just sat there and talked to them on the phone."

"What did I say?"

David remembered it word for word.

"I understand. Yes. I understand. I must go back to Italy. I must be with The Green One. Yes. I understand."

I also repeated a flight number that they had told me, a key detail in the plan to see Fellini. With that I hung up and went back to sleep.

"So, was it them?"

"Yes."

David left L.A. shortly after, a little shaken from just being a witness. Be careful what you wish for, especially when dealing with powers beyond our comprehension.

A few days after he left, I was able to sell the car to the infamous investor Bernie Cornfeld, giving me the cash I needed to make a return trip. The only question was when.

The phone rang. I knew it would be them. I knew they would tell me what I needed. I was growing in not just my fear, but also my understanding of their movements and my connection with them. At least, that's what I was telling myself.

"You are to stand in front of Café Greco on November first at midnight. You will receive more instructions there."

Café Greco was in Rome. That answered that.

Chapter 17

MIDNIGHT AT CAFÉ GRECO AND AN ACT OF DEFIANCE

It had been decided for me. I was so excited that I wanted to call Federico and Eugenio right away…but then I had a thought.

I had been warned not to contact Eugenio. Also, I had not been given any specific instructions as it pertained to Fellini. I was simply told a place to be on a specific date and time. I had acknowledged the call, but didn't say when I was going or where to anyone. And I wasn't going to. Up until this point, for about a year, I had simply served as a willing participant. Everyone else in the group still had some doubts (with maybe the exception of Fellini). Sure they had witnessed phone calls and events that led them to believe we might be dealing with something out of the ordinary, but there was still confusion and skepticism. There were still some lingering feelings that a group or an individual might be behind this, pulling the strings of some elaborate plot.

So I decided not to tell anyone my plans. I kept everything to myself. I got a plane ticket and took off without telling a soul. I flew into Fiumicino and took a cab into the center of Rome. I chose a different hotel, opting for Hotel Raphael, a charmingly old-fashioned yet elegant lodging a short distance from both the popular Piazza Navona and Café Greco. To further protect my anonymity, I had the bellhop show me several different rooms, feigning an inability to choose. I made the poor lad crazy with my indecision, but finally settled on Room 303, a quaint but luxurious space that would suit my needs of both comfort and discretion. I thanked him and tipped him generously, fully confident that I had not been seen or followed.

As soon as he walked out the door, the phone rang.

"We are glad you are here. We will be with you. We are watching you."

How? Just how?! Honestly, I'm not even sure why I was questioning it at this point, but I was intrigued yet again. On a whim, I called the hotel's switchboard operator and asked if the call came from inside or outside the hotel or if it was local or long distance.

"Signorina, I have not connected your line to any call."

I didn't have a lot of time to contemplate this latest mystery as I had a midnight appointment to keep. I had a hunch that something big was going to happen here outside Café Greco. I wasn't sure why, but these instructions were a little more specific. They weren't the vague, *"You must be with The Green One."* There was now a specific time and place, much like when Fellini received his calls. I felt that something in this unusually dysfunctional multi-universe relationship might be changing.

I put on a pink dress (of course) with a black trench coat over the top and left my hotel at around 11:15 to take the short walk, constantly looking over my shoulder to make sure nobody was following me. The streets were all empty; not a soul, not even a moving car. All the shutters of the apartments along the poorly lit streets were shut and locked tight for the night. There was just me and, I'll be honest, I suddenly felt scared. As I stood under the Café Greco sign, I leaned against the wall and held my trench coat closed tight. It was cold that night. I looked like a prostitute waiting for a john. My mind raced and suddenly I had thoughts of You landing its spaceship and taking me up and away. Honestly, I started wondering if I was ready for that. The mind plays its tricks best in the eerie silence of night. I suddenly remembered that no one, not even my family or Federico knew where I was. This was crazy. This was a bad idea. I was about to head back to the hotel.

Somewhere in the distance, a clock struck midnight.

Suddenly, down the street, a few blocks away, I saw a man turn onto Via dei Condotti. He was walking slowly with his head down and his hands in his pockets. There was no one else but him. Who could this be? Is he part of this? Is this who I'm supposed to meet? Could it possibly be You?! Oh my God, what if it…

Wait, it's Andrea! The Blue One!

When Andrea looked up and saw me waving with enthusiasm, he turned white as a ghost. He probably thought I was a ghost!

"What the hell are you doing here? Why are you following me?"

I just sighed. I thought we were past this, but Andrea was never really one for niceties or surprises, for that matter.

I told him how The Voice had told me to be here at this time and to wait for some kind of message. I told him it must have something to do with him.

"No way, that's impossible," he said. "No one knows I am in Rome. I am supposed to be in Milano and that's where I am heading now if I can only remember where I parked my car. I have been combing the streets looking for it and I can't remember where I left it."

He started to tell me about an affair he was having with this actress in Rome and some issues with his girlfriend in Milano. While I listened and offered my support, I also felt that I needed to convince him to stay with me for a bit and wait for a sign.

"There has to be more, Andrea. This isn't a coincidence."

He paused and weighed his words carefully.

"You're right, it's too mysterious," he finally said. "This has to be a sign."

We went back to my hotel and stayed up until the early hours of morning, talking and waiting. We actually reflected back on the trip to Tulum and even entertained theories of how, while we had accepted You was something not of this world, it still might have been tied in with Don Juan. When Andrea decided to take a quick shower, You called to remind me that none of this had to do with Castaneda.

Of course, Andrea didn't believe that he had missed the call.

We talked a little about Eugenio and my feelings for him and The Voice's warning to stay away and the conflict it was causing in me. Andrea told me how Eugenio had grown even more curious about You and our adventures together, getting assurances from all involved, including Andrea himself that these things did in fact happen.

"So you believe?" I asked him, wondering which Andrea had been talking to Eugenio, the one who wrote me the magical, enthusiastic letter or the one who tried to convince Fellini I was a deviant prankster pulling one over on him.

"I don't know. I really don't know," he said.

When I woke up, he was gone, off to find his car and settle things with his girlfriend. Once again, here was I, taking a bold move, flying across the world to follow very specific instructions and for what?

"For what?!" I screamed up to the heavens.

Ring.

"You must be patient."

Click.

I was losing my patience with *patient*. I wanted answers. I wanted meaning, purpose. I had followed every instruction, accepted every single thing they had told me, went forth on blind faith. I had been the only devout follower. And I was continually getting beaten down, frustrated with roadblock after roadblock.

Many years later, I would think of these phone calls and the answers they did give me, the visions I had in my dreams, the amazing miracles I did witness and I would curse my ignorance. You had already shown me a lot up to this point, but I was naive to it. I wanted something more concrete, simpler, easier to understand. I wanted them to answer the easy questions, the burning ones:

Why were they here and what the hell were they, really?

You apparently didn't think I was ready.

I needed to talk to someone else, so I called Fellini, who was as delighted that I was in Rome as he was irritated that I hadn't let him know. After I relayed what had happened, he told me to come see him immediately.

"Christina, we must look for the answers together."

I also lamented to him about my desire to once again see Eugenio and You's instructions to leave him alone. This too frustrated Fellini. He ranted and raved about how Eugenio was a good young man.

"I don't understand why they would have a problem with this," he yelled, passionately. Fellini was now and always going to be a father figure in my life. "This has nothing to do with them. They tell us to do things, to do their bidding and they give us nothing, *nothing* in return. After all this time, we still have no idea who they are and what they want. It's all getting to be ridiculous!"

I had seen bits and pieces of Federico's frustrations with The Voice over the past year. While still intrigued, he was losing his patience at an even faster rate. The proof was in his work. It had now become crystal clear that The Voice wanted him to make a film to spread their message, or however we interpreted that message and the answers we hoped were yet to come. Instead, he wrapped himself up completely in *Ginger and Fred,* a production that had absolutely nothing to do with our adventures together. In fact, this film, a dramedy parody of commercial television and our celebration of entertainers, was probably the furthest thing from what You wanted.

I heard several excuses, all from Fellini himself. First of all, Fellini said he had already committed to *Ginger and Fred* and wanted to honor that commitment, an excuse that, based on his past reputation with productions, didn't really carry any weight. He also said he couldn't find "the story" about our adventures together. He knew there was an interesting event or series of events that had occurred, but he couldn't find a story to tie it together. That too seemed like a slim excuse to me as Fellini had never let the concept of "story" get in the way of sharing his visions. He also had some fear, similar to what he experienced with *The Journey of G. Mastorna.* As he got older, the reality of his dreams affected him more and he started to think of them as premonitions. He felt something in his subconscious was keeping him away from sharing this tale.

Mainly, I think it was out of his stubbornness. He was il Maestro. He didn't like to be told what to do. He also was tired of playing the game. You had given us only a few answers, nothing even close to satisfying Fellini, and he was going to take a defiant stand. He was not going to make this film until he had received more.

He too was frustrated with The Voice.

Over the next several days, I settled into Rome, spending time with Fellini and questioning, once again, why I was even here. I saw Fellini acting defiantly in his own way. Now, I wanted to as well. There was someone else I wanted to see in Rome and I could no longer think of a reason not to see him. This seemed like a wasted trip. Seeing Eugenio would make it worth my while. To hell with the instructions. To hell with The Voice.

To hell with You.

Chapter 18

THE POWER OF THE VOICE

Eugenio was what I like to call "movie star handsome." He was tan and well-built with a full head of hair and he carried himself with full confidence and swagger. He also had another quality that I soon learned attracted me: He was difficult. He exemplified the classic Italian temper and didn't ever really do anything he didn't want to do. He was stubborn and brash...and I loved every bit of it!

After the first trip, we hadn't really kept in contact with each other, even though we both wanted to. I was afraid of You, and he, despite all of his instincts, respected my wishes, even if he didn't understand what I was talking about. Aliens? Voices? This woman might be mad! At one point, I did write him a letter and sent it along with a wristwatch. I had a friend deliver it, testing my limits with The Voice and its ever-watchful eye. Eugenio then sent me a tape recording of his voice talking to me, which melted my heart.

The moment I made the decision to go see him, I received another phone call. This time, I thought to myself, I will stand firm and be defiant. I *would* see Eugenio and The Voice would just have to deal with it. I knew there would be repercussions, but I would handle them. It was about time I started to take a more proactive approach to this relationship and even lay some ground rules. I would let them know that things would now change. I would still listen to them and do what they wanted me to do, but now I wanted answers and a life of my own.

"You may go see him."

That was their short message. I didn't even have to say anything. Perhaps they sensed my frustrations or perhaps they simply didn't want the distraction. Regardless, I immediately rang up Eugenio, who was clearly flustered and frustrated when I told him I had been in Italy and hadn't looked him up. If I was reaching my limits with You, he was done. But You quickly showed it wasn't done with me.

On the second night of our being together, I felt suddenly weary and went to take a nap. My head felt like it was spinning. I was lying down and seemed to be falling asleep, but a terrible panic came upon me. I tried to open my eyes and sit up. I knew I was conscious, but I couldn't move. My eyes were shut tight and the world around me was darkness. Then, like before, I was able to see in my head these tall dark beings around me. As I focused on their faces, the image began to swivel and shift with a blending of colors. It was You. They were here to see me once again. But this time, there was something more intimidating, almost aggressive about their presence. I assumed right away it was because of my recent anger and defiance. I was terrified and yet, I couldn't move or turn away. They stood close and stared into my face, looking me in the eye as I did the same. Nothing was said, but then I *felt* their intention.

"You cannot be afraid. You must stay strong. Stay still. Stay centered. You are The Pink One."

I woke screaming and jumped out of bed, running into the other room and into the arms of Eugenio.

"I am so scared of all of this," I said, breaking down. I was utterly exhausted. It was all getting to be too much. I was still intrigued and I still truly believed I was fulfilling a deeper purpose by listening to The Voice, but it had now taken up more than a year of my life. I had been obsessed by it and really nothing else and all I had to show for it was frustration and terror. Eugenio could only comfort me so far, not understanding what was happening and deeply angered that this experience was clearly taking its toll on me.

During this time, Federico and I grew closer. We were both confused by the randomness of You. We considered what You wanted and how we could satisfy their needs, while still maintaining a sense of normalcy. We talked about what that would involve, how dangerous it might be, how important it might be, and so on. We tried to come up with a plan.

We also talked about the others in the group and how they were now starting to fade away from this adventure. I had first come to Italy to unify The Colors and get us back on track, thinking that was my mission. It was clear that wasn't going to happen. There was still some involvement from some of Fellini's inner circle, but for them, it was more of a fun adventure they didn't really understand. They hadn't experienced the sheer power and the drain of the constant phone calls and demands. Andrea, who we both thought was once a key to this whole thing himself, was fading away from Fellini. Even though he and I had recently had a pleasant evening together, it was clear he would never be fully convinced or committed to anything involving You. Little did we know that during this time he was also writing a fictionalized version of our adventures that would paint Fellini and myself in a poor light and fracture that relationship forever. Others in the group had ceased hearing from The Voice…if they ever had at all. If I was being honest, there was no group. If my job was to unify, I had failed.

Then You told us something that still haunts me to this day. To be honest, I don't know if I believe what they said. I couldn't accept it at the time. Neither could Fellini. It was too painful and overwhelming a thought. It couldn't be true. I still don't know what I believe, whether it was true or simply a "scare tactic" from The Voice in a desperate attempt to play on our human emotions and get us back on track.

In September of that year, just a couple months before my second trip to Italy, there was a devastating earthquake in Mexico City with a magnitude of 8.0 that left more than 5,000 people dead. It was one of the country's most horrific tragedies and a clear reminder of both the power of nature and the fragility of human life.

The Voice said we were responsible.

As Fellini and I talked about the fractured group and our doubts and frustrations, he received a call. You told him that we had been introduced and infused with a powerful energy as a group and as such, we had a responsibility to build that energy together. The constant bickering, the doubt, the anger, the frustration all negated that energy and molded it into something dangerous. You told Fellini that because we had turned this energy into something negative, we created a ripple effect that had caused the earthquake in Mexico City. You essentially told us that our human emotions had ended the lives of thousands of people.

As I write this, I still can't really bring myself to believe that. It just doesn't make sense to me…but then again, none of this ever did. I think You was trying yet another way to scare us back together, to let us know they were in control and that we had to listen to them and do what they asked. If we didn't, there would repercussions, whether real or imagined, small or grand.

"How dare they? How dare they?! Just because we won't do what they want! Because we don't understand them?"

I had never seen Fellini so incensed. He took a greater meaning from the call. He thought You was essentially telling us in veiled words that if we didn't do what they wanted us to do, You had the power to make terrible things happen. Fellini believed them. He could not be convinced that this had anything to do with the energy we created, but rather was a direct result of us not acquiescing to You's demands. It angered him. It terrified me.

Again, I still wasn't sure what I believed, but if there was even the slightest chance that our defiance could cause something so deadly, so horrific, whether caused directly by us or by a stern and angry You, I wanted to be nothing but compliant.

I would encourage Fellini to be the same. There was now more at stake. This was no longer, in my eyes, simply an exciting adventure. It was time to fully do what You wanted us to do and The Pink One was going to once again be there for support and unity. I had a good man in Eugenio to support me. I had the strong bond with Federico. I had the strength and will power and now the fear to motivate me. Over the next couple months, I flew back and forth, and then, finally, I went to Italy and stayed, ready to buckle down and get to the heart of what You wanted.

Chapter 19

SHARING THE STORY

With each visit, Federico and I grew closer. It was during these trips that I first noticed some resistance Fellini was having toward The Voice and its demands, which concerned me and further emphasized my need to stay in Italy permanently.

As if I needed another sign, one came in the form of my stolen car. Not long before I moved to Rome, I received a call from the police informing me that they had finally found my stolen BMW abandoned in the desert. For anyone who has ever had their car stolen, there is an almost sick feeling that comes when you actually find the car again, a sense of violation. We often grow attachments to our vehicles as they are literally with us on our journeys. This BMW had gotten me to L.A. It had taken me out to receive this universal adventure. It was part of the story and now, here I was, standing off an isolated road, looking at nothing but its desecrated shell. My car had been sitting in the desert, rusting in the hot sun. It was stripped bare, all the windows broken, all the tires gone, everything from the inside taken out.

All except for three very special silver coins that were sitting there waiting for me on the front seat.

When I first tossed the I Ching with Fellini, I had used these three coins, all coincidentally from the year 1942, the same year Fellini married his beloved Giulietta. That had resonated with Federico and in all the times that followed in which I tossed the coins for him, he demanded I use these particular ones. These coins were important to me, just as important as my old tarot deck that I had discovered in an antique store many years prior. I had mourned the loss of these coins as much, if not more, than I had mourned the loss of my car. Now here they were waiting for me. To think that nothing else survived from this theft but these three little coins was overwhelming to me and I cried. I knew that they were powerful and I would soon be tossing these for Federico once again. In fact, in the rest of our time together, I would never use another set. I still use them today.

In March of 1986, I moved to Italy to live with Eugenio and to be by Federico's side. I moved for both my own personal happiness and for the deeper mission. Both were equally important. Finally, after all this time, I felt at home. Eugenio and I first stayed in multiple villas provided by the Contessa. Later, we got an apartment of our own on the outskirts of the city central, right in front of the famous Italian fortress Casal de Pazzi. The castle, with its two high towers, got its name from the first and one of the most prominent crusaders of the knights (de Pazzi), who fought in the siege of Jerusalem and returned with three splinters of the holy sepulcher. Its family crest bears three moons and two dolphins. I suppose it was a crazy crusade and I found it ironic that his last name translated to "crazy." I also found it fitting that in my own adventures, I would settle here. Every morning, I got to sip my coffee and look out upon the "Castle of the Crazy" and I found it a fitting guidepost in this adventure.

Settling in Rome proved to be an easy transition for me. I was comfortable here. I had my love and my mentor. I had purpose. Plus, when I first moved out there, The Voice went relatively silent for a time. I always thought that perhaps You was finally content that I had permanently moved closer to The Green One as they had been requesting for years. I thought the next phase of our mission would show itself soon enough. For now, I was content to enjoy the silence and settle into this new life.

During this time, however, The Voice was not leaving Fellini alone. In fact, the demands that he do something with our story were increasing and it was bothering him more and more. When we talked, he would tell me just how invasive and insistent You was being. Federico was still being his stubborn, defiant self, simply hoping that The Voice would eventually yield. He knew better. I soon discovered that not only did The Voice continue to badger him about sharing our adventures and making this film, they also got deeply personal, perhaps as a way to get under his skin and re-establish their power and control…as well as to quell any residual doubt. Sometimes they would use me. One incident that I remember is The Voice telling me how Fellini's son had died, knowing I would share it with Fellini. It was something that deeply hurt Federico and terrified him when I told him. The Voice, while emotionless itself, could be deeply cruel.

Fellini was still hesitant about the film for all his many reasons. But he wasn't necessarily afraid to share the *story,* at least not with those closest to him. That's how Vincenzo Mollica came to be part of the adventure. Vincenzo is still a well-known Italian journalist and writer who was also a close confidant of Fellini's as well as a big fan. In fact, Vincenzo compiled a relatively popular look into the life and art of il Maestro called *Fellini: Words and Drawings.* Vincenzo had interviewed Fellini several times, earning the trust of a man who had a thorny relationship with the media, to say the least. At some point upon his return from the States, Fellini shared stories of our adventures together with Vincenzo, who was deeply intrigued.

Surprised by Fellini's hesitancy to make this wild adventure into a film, Vincenzo still expressed his belief that the story itself was too intriguing not to share. When he spoke with me and I confirmed Fellini's tales, he was even more excited. Somewhere in these discussions, the idea came up to release tales of the adventure in a series of short stories, a serial of sorts in Italy's top newspaper, *Corriere della Sera.* Fellini would have creative control, offering his version of the events with Vincenzo serving as the objective journalist, a voice that gave a unique perspective on the experience. But Fellini was a visual artist so a series of newspaper articles wouldn't be enough. There had to be a visual element.

135

The pair turned to the influential artist Milo Manara, who looked up to Fellini and his approach to art, style, and his career. Though there was a rather large age gap of twenty-five years, the pair had tremendous respect for each other. Milo had built his reputation illustrating for magazines, newspapers, and literary works all over Europe and was growing an international following, one that continues to this day. Milo was introduced into Fellini's inner circle, starting a friendship and partnership that would continue until Fellini's death. This powerful trio worked together to create a six-part look at our adventure that would be called *Trip to Tulum*.

Fellini shared (and directed), Vincenzo wrote, and Milo illustrated all six parts, appearing each day on the front pages of *Corriere della Sera*. The newspaper, eager to carry this new offering from Fellini, hyped the series as a unique sneak peek into the genius's creative process, stating, "For the first time, the great director reveals the plot of his next film."

Fellini didn't argue it, unsure of what would come from the series. Would it be well-received? Would it offer clarity, perspective, perhaps even closure? Would it push him to do something more with the tale or would its telling suffice? Would it become a film? Would it satisfy The Voice? What would happen now? These were all questions Fellini had for me as we read tarot or tossed coins together every day at his office. The answers were often left unclear. The only option was to go forward and see where the series took him.

Fellini surprised us all by announcing that the series was all true. However, nothing with Fellini could really be taken at face value. The series was definitely a *fantastical* look at our adventures; a creative, symbolic interpretation of what happened and what Federico found most important.

To try and sum up in a paragraph or two the art, beauty, and symbolism of *Trip to Tulum* wouldn't be doing it justice and would take away from its power. It is a Fellini-esque fiction, a look at our events together blended with elements of pure fantasy as well as moments of clear truth. It is Fellini's own take on not just the players

From our interview to Tullio Pinelli

I started to work with Fellini and a few days after I received the first phone call. I'd been waiting for it anxiously and the text I gave you is about it. From that day I have received a series of eight phone calls. The first two or three were very affectionate, in a protective tone, I wouldn't say threatening but after all… "…do it this way because it's better for you and because you should feel free about what you're doing instead of telling the story as a chronicle".

At that time we were working and we were close to finishing this project, which was mainly a chronicle of what Fellini told about the things that happened. During one of the phone calls that followed (I have told those persons right away that I wasn't scared at all, and that instead I was very curious) the first thing they told me was that a sort of a chain has been formed, not magic, but something similar, with a series of colors that they have assigned to each component of the group. And Fellini was green. Strange, but when I met Rol the first time, he told me that green has always been the color that enclosed the secret of the divine power that surrounds us. Green is the fifth musical note, and those persons spoke of it as of a magic color. Then, there was an American girl that I met later on, who was pink. Filippo was white and De Carlo was blue. They assigned the violet color to me, perhaps because the other colors were finished (he laughs).

Anyway, during all these telephonic relationships they have strangely insisted, and in a very heavy way, about the importance of these colors, which, according to them, formed a sort of a magic chain that had to be respected by common accord of all the colors. In case of contrasts or fractures, very great dangers were going to occur. They were very constant and peremptory about this, I never understood why…

From Pinelli's notes after one of the phone call of the Voices

Telephone call received on June 6th, 1986.
From10:00 Am. to 10:40 Am.

A long and particularly important conversation. The beginning is the usual: a weak, wheezy voice, of which I can understand only the words "Color Violet". Then it becomes clear.
- "We know that you wish to make some questions."
- "What kind of questions?"
- "Regarding the experience that you have lived."
-" It's true. You must understand that it has been such a unique and unusual experience that we still keep asking ourselves what it really was, why you were so interested in making a film, and who you really are?"

This is the answer that I have summarized, trying to maintain as much as possible the particular and precise phrases they have used.
- "We have some limits in expressing ourselves with you. The most important one stands in our necessity to translate into simple concepts a matter that is not possible to articulate. We try to define the bases of the communication. We have explained to you about the existance of the vital energies, which surround the human bieng and that continue to exist after his death. In that way you should interpret you question concerning the God. Our answer "we are" is to be interpreted on that basis. this does not imply our possibility to decide human actions. In our world there are different levels of entities and levels that are superior to ours. the state in which we are is the closest to yours."
- "From where do you call?"
- "We call from a non physical dimension, but the communication takes place on a physical level"
- "We have often thought with Green that you were a society of parapsychologists or beings endowed with strong paranormal powers, yet always human beings."
"It is not a society; but the Voice, which expresses the concepts that we try to communicate to you, belongs to beings endowed with human vocal capabilities; but those beings are not conscious while they talk."
- "It means that you are non-human entities who, in order to talk to us, use human beings who are not conscious of it."
- "That is the exact answer. We have never been incarnated; we are not souls of dead human beings. We cannot wait any longer now (...)

involved, but why we were all there, what our roles were, and how we adventured together. The series also allowed Fellini to get deeply personal, showing his fear, confusion, frustration, and need for partners as he experienced one of the more surreal adventures of his life. Just like his films, *Trip to Tulum* is a dreamscape on which Fellini plays, offering what he wants his followers to see. Lucky for us, as with all of his art, the series allowed a glimpse into his soul.

The series provided only a condensed version of our story. In true Fellini fashion, he brought his tale to a close with even more intrigue, stating:

"I don't know whether I will transfer this narrative to the form of images, or when. But the fact that I accepted the invitation to publish the story before making the film makes me suspect that I was following an unconscious instinct to put it in abeyance. The same instinct tells me that you patient readers who have followed this story to the end should be let in on a little secret: the journey and mysterious adventure that led to this tale, freely told as cinematic narrative, really happened."

When the series broke, there was a lot of speculation about what Fellini would eventually do with this material. There was excitement about the prospects of turning this into a film and, based on the public's reaction, the potential success for that film. Perhaps this could be the one that snapped Fellini out of his artistic funk. The public was already showing they had an interest in the story and Fellini was already working with a great creative team who seemed ready to help him translate this into any medium. There was excitement by everybody involved...

...except for me. Call it instinct, intuition, whatever. I had a gut feeling Fellini was not going make this film. Once he offered our story in this way, I knew it would be the end of it. Fellini was a man who jumped from project to project. Once he felt his story was told, he was on to the next one. He had also been torn for a few years now on what he wanted to do with this particular story, balking at almost every chance to make the film. He had often blatantly ignored The

Voice, even when it was at its most intrusive and terrifying. Fellini did things his way. He found a vehicle through which he would be comfortable sharing our adventures and that was how he was going to do it, no matter what anyone said. He was steadfast and defiant.

I was scared.

I had a hunch this wouldn't satisfy You. Things didn't go well when we didn't follow their directions exactly. During this process, while The Voice was leaving me be, You was still calling Fellini.

And this time, they were clear.

"This is not what we ask of you."

Fellini chose to ignore You and go forward, despite repeated warnings. At some point in the process, The Voice once again turned to the people in his circle to get Fellini back on track. We were never quite sure why, but we suspected either Fellini had relented at some point and offered the possibility of turning this into something bigger and The Voice knew he needed our support or he had gone the exact opposite route, refusing to listen to You's demands and they thought Fellini now needed our influence.

The calls once again came, not just to me, but now others in his inner circle, including his good friend Tullio Pinelli. Tullio was a meticulous man who, despite his early reservations about Fellini's tale, accepted the presence of You and his involvement. Fellini had gone to Tullio with his frustrations throughout this process, from his indecision of what to do with the story of this adventure and the demands of this alien voice, all the way through its apparent dissatisfaction with the series. There was even speculation that Fellini, in one of his weaker moments, possibly talked to Tullio about potentially writing a screenplay to turn into a film if The Voice wouldn't relent, though I never got a confirmation on this.

Still, suddenly Tullio was intimately involved in our adventure, receiving a series of calls, more than the rest of us were receiving at that time, except for maybe me and Fellini himself. He told us that the nature of these calls, for the most part, was designed to get us to encourage and guide Fellini in a certain way.

"*This is way better for you. For him. For all.*"

To his credit, Tullio was never scared, but was curious and eager to play his part. He was called The Violet One, though we already had a Violet One in Brinke. That being said, Brinke hadn't received a call in years so perhaps, we thought, she had been replaced. He was told, like me, to stay close to The Green One and to help him. He was told of the importance of colors and our role in a greater adventure. Perhaps, because he was so open, he was also given a glimpse into You's purpose. Tullio was a detailed man and he took notes on his calls from The Voice, offering at least a hint of clarity all these years later:

From Tullio's notes: June 6, 1986 at 10 a.m.

Tullio started by asking who they were.

"*We have some limits in expressing ourselves with you. The most important one stands in our necessity to translate into simple concepts a matter that is not possible to articulate. We try to define the basis of the communication, we explained to you about the existence of the vital energies, which surround the human being and that continue to exist after his death. In that way, you should interpret your question concerning God. Our answer 'we are' is to be interpreted on that basis. This does not imply our possibility to decide human actions. In our world, there are different levels of entities and levels that are superior to ours. The state in which we are is the closest to yours.*"

Tullio then asked where they are calling from.

"*We call from a non-physical dimension but the communication takes place on a physical level.*"

He then asked the big question…who they were.

"*It is not a society, but the voice, which expresses concepts that we try to communicate with you, belongs to beings endowed with human vocal capabilities. But those beings are not conscious while they talk… we have never been incarnated. We are not souls of dead human beings. We are something else.*"

Then later, they offered the most ominous message.

"*We cannot wait any longer now!*"

As with all things related to You, these answers simply brought up more questions. You was reaching out to us, trying to offer more in their own vague, confusing way. We were still stuck trying to interpret the message and encourage a man who had grown frustrated, angry, and even bitter toward The Voice and his role in their mission. There was still possibility. After all, Fellini purposely never put "The End" on any of his creative works and he wouldn't do so here either. But something needed to shift. We all felt something was going to happen, we just weren't sure what exactly.

Meanwhile, this series was taking off and for me personally, life was about to change in a very dramatic fashion. I wondered going forward, how was I going to balance these new changes and fulfilling my *human* purpose, while also working on my universal purpose as The Pink One.

PER LA PRIMA VOLTA IL GRANDE REGISTA RACCONTA IL SUO PROSSIMO FILM (VERSIONE DELLO STESSO FELLINI E DI TULLIO PINELLI)

VIAGGIO A TULUN

di FEDERICO FELLINI

Disegni di Milo Manara

Corriere Della Sera, *Viaggio A Tulum* (Trip to Tulum)

VIAGGIO A TULUN / PER LA PRIMA VOLTA IL GRANDE REGISTA RACCONTA IL SUO PROSSIMO FILM

I MESSAGGI DELLA VOCE MISTERIOSA

di FEDERICO FELLINI

Disegno di Milo Manara

Corriere Della Sera. *I Messaggi Della Voce Misteriosa* (Mysterious Messages from the Voice)

«I BARRACUDA? NON POSSONO FARCI NIENTE»

di FEDERICO FELLINI

disegno di Milo Manara

RIASSUNTO DELLE PUNTATE PRECEDENTI — 3

Corriere Della Sera, *I Barracua? Non Possono Farci Niente* (Barracudas? They can't do anything to you!)

ALLA RICERCA DELLA PIETRA OTTAGONALE

di FEDERICO FELLINI

disegno di Vito Manara

RIASSUNTO DELLE PUNTATE PRECEDENTI

4

Corriere Della Sera, *Alla Ricerca Della Pietra Ottagonale* (In Search of the Octagonal Stone)

Adattamento cinematografico di Federico Fellini

VIAGGIO A TULUN / PER LA PRIMA VOLTA IL GRANDE REGISTA RACCONTA IL SUO PROSSIMO FILM

UN CONCERTO DI DISSONANZE IN RIVA AL MARE

di FEDERICO FELLINI
disegni di Milo Manara

5 — RIASSUNTO DELLE PUNTATE PRECEDENTI — Il regista italiano con un gruppo di persone sta compiendo un viaggio alla ricerca dei luoghi, personaggi, leggende e riti musicali di antiche civiltà andino-americane, descritti nei libri di uno studioso latino-americano. Il viaggio è come guidato da messaggi misteriosi. Diversi i versi i...

[Testo dell'articolo]

Corriere Della Sera, *Un Concerto Di Dissonanze In Riva Al Mare* (A Concert of Dissonances by the Sea)

VIAGGIO A TULUN / PER LA PRIMA VOLTA IL GRANDE REGISTA RACCONTA IL SUO PROSSIMO LAVORO

CHE FILM PROIETTANO SUL JUMBO DEL RITORNO?

di FEDERICO FELLINI
disegno dell'autore

6 RIASSUNTO DELLE PUNTATE PRECEDENTI — Il regista italiano insieme a un gruppo di persone formato da del giornalista Gian Maria, la nasa e sempre più misteriosa Helen e Tobia, sta compiendo un viaggio di esplorazione in un luogo di antiche civiltà.

Corriere Della Sera, *Che Film Proiettano Sul Jumbo Del Ritorno?*
(What Kind of Film Project on this Jumbo Plane Will We Return With?)

Chapter 20

LIFE IN ITALY, LIFE IN THE PAPERS

As popular and revered as Fellini was, I don't think anybody in his camp or even Fellini himself expected this type of reception from Italian readers. Copies of *Corriere della Sera* were flying off the racks and the public was fascinated by il Maestro's latest and perhaps greatest adventure.

As such, Fellini and Manara decided to flesh out the project beyond the six serial entries and produce a more in-depth comic book series through the popular art magazine *Corto Maltese*. For Manara, who was already established in this medium, it was a rare opportunity to bring to life the images and imagination of one of his icons. In later interviews, Manara spoke of the process as "intensive" and yet, also "intimate." He talked about the challenges of bringing Fellini's visions to life in *any* medium and that throughout the process, though this was not film, Fellini was ever the director. Manara accepted his role as a cameraman with a brush rather than a camera.

For Fellini, this expanded project was not only a chance to once again delve back into an old love and his affinity for comic books, it was also, he hoped, enough to satisfy You and take the pressure off of doing a movie.

Once, in an interview, when describing the project, he described, "The notion that seeing the story transformed into a graphic novel would vanquish once and for all any minute remainder of my impetus to make it a film."

Trip to Tulum ran for a year in *Corto Maltese* and then was eventually collected and published as a hardcover graphic novel. Around the same time, Fellini's *Ginger and Fred* was released and became a hit in Italy...despite more criticism internationally. In Italy, Fellini could do no wrong. However, among his devotees and the arthouse critics who once loved and lauded him, he was losing some of that reverence with his recent films.

Plus, Fellini admitted he was still feeling creatively tapped.

As his confidante, he and I had several conversations about the nature of his creative process, his inspiration, and how and why he made films. He was very open and candid with me (on his terms) and he admitted that the creative visions were much more prominent in his younger years. As he got older, he struggled more and more with feelings of self-doubt, frustration, creative blocks, and so on. He thought often of giving up filmmaking, but always talked himself back into it when he realized he still had stories he wanted to tell. The process itself was just getting harder.

"That's why I keep so many people around me, people like you Christina," he said to me one afternoon at his studio as I gave him a reading. "You all give me fresh ideas. You keep my creative process going."

I've always been honored by that.

He talked about how much he liked having creative people in his life...the weirder and wackier the better! We could bring him stories. We could *understand* his stories.

I realize that there is a certain irony here. This legend wanted to share his stories like no one else and yet, You had served one up on a plate for him, one that they were trying to essentially force him to take on and yet, he resisted. I know I already offered up many possible reasons why there was such resistance, but even now, looking back, it's still difficult to comprehend. This whole story seemed to be a perfect setting for the next Fellini masterpiece, one that would re-inspire both him and his critics, one that could get the creative juices flowing again, one that could help make an even bigger mark.

Instead, he began production on the more indulgent and complex film-within-a-film project *Intervista,* a hard look at his thoughts on the process of filmmaking and the struggles he was dealing with as an aging artist. At the time, Fellini took on this film to fulfill a promise to a producer and in part, because it was going to be an easier film to make. Between that and his work on the *Trip to Tulum* project, Fellini kept himself busy… busy enough to ignore the ever-increasing phone calls from You.

Meanwhile, the *Corriere della Sera* articles essentially announced my arrival and my involvement in Fellini's life to the masses. A fictionalized version of me proved to be a central character in Fellini's story; a loving, sexual, free-spirited spiritual guide for Fellini and his compatriots in the series. I was naked in the book, perhaps due to Fellini's appreciation of how open I was, how "transparent" as he used to say. "You have nothing to hide!" As Fellini boasted that this series was all based on true events, readers wondered about this American blonde and that's when they discovered me.

Fellini was never shy about introducing me around and, as such, I became known as "Fellini's girl," not in any kind of sexual way, but rather like a father/daughter relationship. I was young and very good-looking, having kept up my modeling regiment. I was unusually blonde for that part of the world, happy, excited, and connected to Italy's true king of entertainment. As such, I was embraced by Italy and my acting and modeling career took off. I did several commercials, photos shoots, and even took part in some TV shows and films, including Fellini's! That being said, in his films, I was typically cast as "mysterious blonde girl who walks by." Not the most thrilling of roles.

Still, settling into the career I had always wanted and doing it at Fellini's side was beyond exciting. I met with Fellini every day to give him a reading and just to talk. I also got invaluable advice from him on the industry and I know he helped me from time to time with jobs. I spent my days by the side of a genius, exploring my new country and building a life with Eugenio. It was perfect.

As I was Fellini's girl and my stock was beginning to rise, I was invited to appear on both *Indietro Tutta,* a popular variety show, and *The Maurizio Costanzo Show,* a very popular talk show in Italy on par with *The Tonight Show* here in the States. On that show, all of Maurizio's guests—a wide variety of characters—would sit in a semicircle and simply have a discussion about a certain topic or topics, sometimes taking questions from the audience. No matter the topic, I would always turn to my astrology for my contributions. Between that, my looks, a ditsy blonde character persona I took on, how animated and energetic I was, and my mispronunciation of certain Italian words…fans of the show loved me. I had a blast, playing up this character and never caring if the joke was on me. Maurizio was always digging for gossip on Fellini and I had fun playing our version of cat and mouse. Over the next four years, I was invited back more than a dozen times.

As I was settling in, Fellini himself felt more and more unsettled. Even as he eyed his new film project, he knew in his heart he was still defying this higher power and it toyed with his emotions. What's a little ironic about his taking on *Intervista* is that he includes himself as a key character in the film. One of the few times he opened up to me about his hesitancy to do a film on our Tulum adventures, he said one of the reasons he couldn't *see* the story was because of his close involvement in it. He didn't want to make a film in which he was the central character. He always wanted things to happen to characters he created and not to him. Yet, here he was, embarking on the *Intervista* project that was deeply personal. It was confusing. For You, it was frustrating.

Over my first couple years living in Italy, I tried my best to both adhere to The Voice's always confusing demands and support my mentor, the man I respected above all else. We watched and waited, hoping the graphic novel would satisfy You. When it didn't, we pondered what to do next.

Chapter 21

Eight, Eight, Eighty-Eight

During this time, as we struggled with the ever-pressing need of meeting The Voice's demands, I also experienced one of the happiest moments of my life...my wedding to Eugenio. It was one of the most beautiful events I have ever been a part of; a wonderful day, a dream wedding that brought most, if not all, of the people closest to me together, merging of my old life with the new.

You was there too.

In January of 1988, Eugenio proposed to me and I couldn't have been more thrilled. Ever the devotee to the importance of symbols and numbers, I chose 8-8-88 as the date to get married. It seemed fitting for my life and the life we were going to create together. I saw great luck and fortune in those numbers. Plus, Italians, by nature, are very superstitious, at least in my experience. It's bad luck to spill the salt, you can't pass salt from hand to hand, if you spill wine you must dip your finger in it and put it on your wrist or neck, you don't want to see a black cat, if you spill water you put a little wine on top of the water, and so on and so on. One of the earliest mistakes I made with my future mother-in-law was to get her chrysanthemums. She freaked out.

"Those are the flowers for the dead!"

Eugenio's family was very superstitious and believed in the power of numbers as well. Our date seemed perfect.

We chose Basilica de Santa Francesca Romana, right next to the Coliseum as the place to hold our wedding. The church was once used as a place to worship the Roman god Venus in the first century and I felt a great power there. Also, I had a pigeon crap on my head as I went in to look at the church for the first time and an old woman on the street who saw the incident told me it was good luck. I would be blessed if I married there. That sealed the deal.

In the days and months leading up to the wedding, I experienced a few crazy things that sometimes made me question if I was doing the right thing or if my actions were angering someone or something more powerful. First, in April of that year, I flew back to New York to see some old friends and then to New Jersey to see my parents and buy a wedding dress. After dropping a ton of money on a beautiful dress, it was stolen! I was loading my car on the streets of New York, making sure a doorman was watching the car and somehow, somebody still managed to lift it from the car. I was devastated, but had to go back to the store and drop down a good chunk of money for another one. As sensitive as I was to all that was happening in my life over the past few years, I instantly wondered if this was a sign. In fact, if I remember right, I even got so scared that I briefly called off the wedding. However, some Italian coaxing from my soon-to-be mother-in-law brought me back to reality.

I also spent some time with some old friends and acquaintances whose lives had sadly become a mix of drinking, drugs, and all-night benders. I quickly realized, as many of us do as we start new chapters in our lives, that I had little in common with many of them and that it was time to move on. After one night where I almost ended up in the middle of a gun fight between two of them, I realized this was no longer my scene. I was okay with that.

I'd rather spend my time with hot-headed Italians and mind-fucking aliens.

Still, I was able to connect with two dear friends from my life who would fly to Italy and do me the honor of serving as my bridesmaids. My friend Jennifer had known me since we were teenagers and was one of my only true friends in high school. She had been with me all throughout my awkward teen years, into my secret life as a

Federico Fellini and Christina on her wedding day to Eugenio Cappuccio,
August 8, 1988

Wedding day, Eugenio Cappuccio.

model and through a tumultuous relationship with Woody before I met Fellini. Caroline was a friend from my modeling days. She and I experienced what seemed like another life together with some unbelievable adventures, including one time where she essentially had to rescue me from being kidnapped by an Arabian prince in Paris…but that's a story for a different time.

The wedding itself was beautiful. I had friends and relatives from Germany, Spain, London, New York, New Jersey, and L.A., and of course all my new Italian friends and family. The reception was at The Policeman's Club as my new father-in-law was chief of police. The ceremony and reception were filled with love and our location looked like the set of a Fellini film. There were prominent Italian actors and politicians and of course, Fellini himself, who gave me away to my new husband with a hug and a huge smile. It was truly a storybook wedding and a very important day for me, one of the most special moments I ever experienced…and You made its presence felt as well.

It all started the morning of my wedding day when Eugenio finally received a call from The Voice.

I had just finished drawing myself a bath when the phone started ringing. Eugenio was packing his tuxedo and shoes and I could hear him going to answer the phone with an exasperated sigh. The phone had been ringing for the last few weeks with calls from friends, family, caterers, wedding planners, etc. I was glad I was preoccupied and didn't need to take the call. I closed my eyes and tried to get in a few final moments of relaxation before the chaos of the big day. It was eight a.m.

"Christina!"

Eugenio barged into the bathroom.

"What?" I cried out, fearing the worst. Something had gone wrong.

"I just got a call!"

"Yeah, I heard…from who?"

"From them."

And suddenly I knew exactly who he was talking about, and I was relieved. The Voice has been a sore spot between Eugenio and me for almost the entire duration of our relationship. From the moment I told him the story, he was skeptical. Then, when other people in our lives started getting calls or talked about their experiences, that skepticism turned to jealousy and even anger. There was no relationship he was more jealous of than mine and Fellini's. Despite my love for Eugenio, Fellini and I would always have our own unique relationship, built largely upon our experiences with You. I continued to see Fellini every day and this often angered Eugenio. I'm sure it didn't help that Fellini was a well-known Lothario. No matter how many times I assured my future husband that nothing sexual was happening, he was always doubtful. He loved Fellini but didn't like that we had this secret relationship built on something he didn't understand or fully believe. It was a constant strain and I often begged The Voice to simply call him and let him know that this was all real.

"What happened?" I asked, noticing how pale he looked. His face showed me that he had in fact experienced a phone call. I knew that look all too well.

"Well, it sounded like it was a machine," he said. "There was static and a voice that sounded like it was far away and they spoke to me in Italian."

"That was You. What did they say?"

"They…they called me by my name and they said they wished they could be here for us."

I was initially wary of this, especially when I pondered how much they wanted me to stay away from Eugenio at the beginning. What made You change their tune?

"Christina, they told me they were marziani."

Marziani is "Martian" in Italian. There really was no Italian word at the time that translated into "alien." Nowadays, they say "alieno," but a couple decades ago, *marziani* was more often used. You had not only called Eugenio, they also showed him their true colors.

"They said we should look up at the sky tonight at 22:22 and they will give us a sign."

He was teeming with excitement. I soon realized that for Eugenio, 10:22 p.m. might now be the most exciting part of this special day and I was okay with that.

The wedding itself went without a hitch and at about quarter after ten, I snatched Eugenio away from our friends and family and brought him up to the roof of The Policeman's Club. We sat there waiting with great anticipation. Eugenio couldn't sit still, constantly asking me what was going to happen. I could see he expected some grand fireworks and something inside me knew that no matter what, he was going to be disappointed. Eugenio was expecting them to "drop the ladder" as it were and I knew that wasn't going to happen. You was only going to make a small appearance tonight if any at all.

At exactly 22:22 (all combined to equal eight), we looked up to the sky and saw what looked like a plane or a star. Suddenly, it moved rapidly, zig-zagging across the sky. We could see a trail of light and that trail formed a figure eight. With that, it was gone. It took all of five seconds and for me, I thought it was a wonderful sign and a gift. The Voice had accepted this marriage and let me know that they were still here and supported The Pink One's life. It was one of the few times they showed themselves to me where they didn't want anything other than to let me know all was well. It was a perfect ending to my wedding day.

"That's it?!"

Eugenio still looked up to the sky, waiting for them to come back. I knew it.

"Didn't you see the pattern? The eight?" I asked, putting my arm around him.

"That was a plane."

"What kind of plane moves back and forth like that?" I asked.

Eugenio simply stood there staring up at the sky for a few more moments. Finally, he gave up, disappointed that his part in this adventure was only witnessing a few lights. I felt for him as I could see excitement flow out of him. Finally, he simply put his head down, grabbed my hand lovingly and started to walk back downstairs to rejoin our wedding. He would never hear from The Voice again, and he still sometimes questioned the authenticity of mine and Fellini's tales throughout our marriage. For Eugenio, it was a disappointing way to end a glorious day.

For me, it was a rare show of support and a reminder that there was still work to be done, that they were still here…so I thought.

Chapter 22

An American Artist in Italy

Unfortunately, I would soon be distracted once again, this time by my career and a personal life that would prove to be anything but the romantic fantasy I had dreamed about with Eugenio.

My new husband and I didn't have a honeymoon, or *luna di miele*, as the Italians call it because we were both wrapped up in projects in our entertainment careers. Eugenio was working on wrapping up a film project with the Italian director Pasquale Squitieri, known for some regionally popular spaghetti westerns and later some politically charged, socially engaging Italian films that sparked controversy in his homeland. Squitieri had also just cast me as a supporting character in his next film, *Russicum* (*The Third Solution*) to start shooting in Rome at the end of the year.

Before that project, I was cast as a lead in a new film by Roger Vadim, who was an established theatre and film writer and director and the man who brought the cult classic *Barbarella* to the masses. He was known more for his legendary romances, including marriages to both Brigitte Bardot and Jane Fonda. He was an extremely handsome, charming, and passionate man and I was thrilled that he had tagged me for his next film, knowing full well what this could mean for my career. As we went through pre-production meetings, I grew more and more excited about a project that had me trying on multiple costumes and wigs, attempting to get the exact look he wanted for the film. He even told me to gain some weight, to add some curves to my model's body. The look he was going for was close to Barbarella, but with a new twist and I was having fun with the idea of the outlandish style.

Knowing my head would be covered, I decided to completely switch things up with my own look. I chopped off a lot of my hair and dyed the rest black. I'm not really sure why I made such a drastic change but I think I was feeling like I wanted to do something extreme. It was extreme alright, completely changing how I looked in every possible way. For the time, it was a bold look, very mod, very Eastern European and extremely stylish.

My husband hated it.

This was yet another thing for Eugenio and me to argue about. As I said, we didn't have a honeymoon and I mean that in many ways. While the courting and the wedding day were beyond compare, highlighted by an unexpected visit and a breath-taking sign by You, the magic and wonder of the romance very quickly started to fade. It didn't help that just days after our wedding, Eugenio informed me how he both never wanted kids and that he was a womanizer who would struggle to be faithful to me.

Not the words you want to hear from your new husband.

There was also still the tension that existed between my husband and me over my relationship with Fellini, whom he idolized. Eugenio was a talented artist in his own right, but to follow in the footsteps of one of the greats is an exercise in frustration and our closeness continued to cause feelings of jealousy that extended beyond mere talent.

I continued to not only do readings for Fellini but also others in the Italian elite, including the girlfriends of the former Prime Minister Bettino Craxi and his right hand man Claudio Martelli. We all became very close friends and would travel and explore together, even taking some luxurious vacations on their yachts, private jet meetings with international dignitaries, and high-profile parties. Eugenio was jealous of these relationships as well, but we eventually included him. In fact, after some coaxing by me, Claudio hired Eugenio to do some publicity work for their Socialist Party. Eugenio agreed to direct a series of five propaganda commercials for the party, leading up to the next voting cycle. When Claudio and his party won, we were handed a literal suitcase full of money, more than we had ever seen.

The hair incident continued to chip away at the cracks in our relationship, however. Not long after we were married, Eugenio and I went to the Venice Film Festival to show support for Squitieri, who was nominated for a film in which Eugenio was assistant director. I originally thought we could use this trip as the honeymoon we never had, but Eugenio didn't want to be seen with me as long as I had this new hair style. He wanted his American woman with long, blonde hair…and he would be able to find her at the festival. As he hunted at the festival, I mainly stayed at the hotel, depressed and starting to wonder what I was doing with this relationship.

"What the hell did you do with your hair?!"

That was the explosion from Vadim as I showed up at his studio to prepare for the next phase of pre-production for what would be my breakout role.

"Well, I wanted to do something different," I said, startled by his reaction. "I needed a change and I thought it wouldn't really matter since I'm wearing a wig anyway."

"I decided against the wig and now you show up with this?!"

He was livid. I could feel my heart sink. This was not a good way for us to start and I was worried. He soon confirmed my fears.

"Christina, you better show up tomorrow with blonde hair or you're fired."

Wonderful.

I ran to the nearest hairdresser, desperately asking if there was anything we could do. As we began the process of trying to "fix" my hair, it was soon apparent that doing the multiple dye jobs so closely together was going to do some major damage. Sure enough, large chunks of my hair started falling out and the blonde wasn't enough to cover the dark color…the result was a yellowish orange. We had to trim away even more and suddenly I was looking like Annie Lennox. It was the best we could do.

I was subsequently fired from the film and my husband could

hardly stand to even look at me. It was devastating and depressing.

"I don't care what you look like Christina, as long as you're happy."

The Green One was always there when I needed him the most. Perhaps he could sense I was struggling and was simply being kind or perhaps he truly meant what he said. Whatever his reasons, the words of my mentor meant so much to me during this dark time. As I struggled more and more with my marriage and depression, it was comforting to know that he was there for me, helping me as I tried to figure out what to do next.

The answer soon came and ironically enough, it was because of my hair. My modeling agency absolutely *loved* the look. It turns out, so did Italian media. Soon I was doing commercials for luxury cars, orange juice, tuna fish, cough drops, and more. I was doing more print work and even appeared in some Italian telenovelas, along with my work on *The Maurizio Costanzo Show*. With my new look, I was now truly the wacky American psychic and I played it up (and ate it up) as much as I could.

Money started rolling in, which helped ease the tension between me and Eugenio. He even started to adapt to my hair style, though it was still a talking point. He and I made a film together called *La Americana* about a sweet American psychic in Rome. I also shot *Russicum*, playing a double agent with an edge. With this new look, I started to get cast as villains or "tough-gals" as opposed to the girl next door or the ditzy California blonde.

It was actually more exciting.

For a time, things were good, but there was something unsettling about it all that I couldn't put my finger on. Something didn't feel right, even as I felt like my personal life was finally easing into a comfort I hadn't known for a while. One morning as I prepared to go to visit Fellini, it hit me. I hadn't thought about The Voice in weeks, if not months.

Even more disturbing, You hadn't called.

Chapter 23

The Colors Fade

I hadn't heard anything from The Voice since my wedding night.

Even though the sign itself was beautiful and I really appreciated their reaching out to show Eugenio they were real, it certainly didn't feel like any kind of closure. Why would it? We still hadn't fulfilled their request. We hadn't completed our mission. In fact, if anything, we were getting further away from what they wanted us to do. We were getting further away from helping Fellini fulfill his destiny. We were getting further away from each other.

I couldn't help but feel responsible.

After all, I was The Pink One. I was the unifier, the catalyst. I was the blend of colors. If Fellini was their artist, I was their conduit… and we were no longer communicating. We weren't collaborating. We were really *nothing*. What had happened? How had we let this all go? Over the course of five or six years, life was definitely going to carry on and even sometimes get in the way, but how had we drifted so far off our mission? Would we be able to recover? Would The Voice still want to use us? Was there even a mission?

What, if anything, was going to happen next?

These thoughts plagued me in the months after the wedding. Whereas I once hoped and prayed The Voice would leave me be, I now discovered that in a twisted way, I missed its presence. Well, perhaps I didn't miss it, but after being such a presence for so long, I now wasn't sure what to do without You and its demands. As soon as they were gone, I had time to reflect even further as to how important

Christina Engelhardt aus Rom

Das schöne Orakel der Stars

Sie prophezeite dem Kinderfeind Woody Allen ein Baby – und behielt recht. Seitdem setzt halb Hollywood auf die übersinnlichen Kräfte der blonden Hexe

Star-Regisseur Woody Allen lief krebsrot an und brüllte im Zorn: „Was erlauben Sie sich – ich hasse Babys!" Ein achtlos dahergesagter Satz einer schönen Blondine hatte den Künstler derart in Rage versetzt: „Sie werden demnächst Vater, Mr. Allen." Außerdem hatte er doch gar nicht mit der jungen Dame ... Was die pikante Vorhersage der Christina Engelhardt, Darstellerin einer Schönheitskönigin in Allens „Stardust Memories", wirklich bedeutete, ging allen Beteiligten wenig später auf. Nach langer, fruchtloser Lebensgemeinschaft wurde Allens Freundin Mia Farrow von ihrem Partner schwanger.

Das für den Regisseur am Ende vielleicht doch noch freudige Ereignis begründete Christina Engelhardts heute legendären Ruf als „Orakel der Stars". Die deutschstämmige Schauspielerin (geboren 1961

York) mit Wohnsitz Rom zu QUICK: „Ich bin eine moderne Hexe, kann oft sogar in die Zukunft sehen. So viele meiner Vorhersagen sind eingetroffen, daß manche Künstler keine wichtige Entscheidung treffen, ohne mich vorher zu befragen."

Kultfilmemacher Federico

Künstlerin Claudia Cardinale: Sie ließ sich

Starb Federico Fellini: Der Meisterregisseur war aus Dankbarkeit so treue Dienste Trauzeuge, als Christina am 9. 9. 1988 TV-Präsident Eugenio heiratete

Fellini („8 1/2") etwa fährt bei Dreharbeiten aus Vorsicht nur noch U-Bahn, seit ihm Christina, die studierte Psychologin (US-Uni Princeton) „einen Autounfall während der Arbeit" vorhersagte. Hollywood-Tycoon Francis Coppola engagierte das ehemalige Fotomodell (1,73 Meter, 55 Kilo, grüne Augen) für den Film „Der Pate III" – um die Produktion mit einem Voodoo-Ritual vor Mafia-Anschlägen zu schützen. Auch „Rocky" Sylvester Stallone erlag der Faszination der

Gürtel im Taekwondo): Er läßt Christina die Qualität von Drehbüchern, per Pendel prüfen. Und Kino-Diva Claudia Cardinale setzt bei Finanzfragen auf Christinas Vorhersage-Künste.

Berühmte Klienten, großer Ruhm – trotzdem ist die Star-Hexe mit den vielen Talenten nicht grenzenlos glücklich. „Mir fehlt die unschuldige Freude über Komplimente eines Mannes, die normale Frauen empfinden", klagt Christina. „Ein Blick in seine Augen, und ich weiß, was er von mir will."

German magazine *Quick*, 1989.

On the set with Federico Fellini

On the set with Federico Fellini (Photo: Francesco Escalar)

our mission might have been, how special we were to have been chosen and sadly, how we might have thrown it all away because of the trivialities of life circumstances, ego, and miscommunication. I was sad that The Voice had suddenly, after so much time, seemed to give up on us. Was their sign on my wedding night actually them leaving? I was also worried that there would be a more final, severe goodbye. Would You just leave us alone with what we had experienced or would there be a silencing. Perhaps I was being overly paranoid, but I could never predict what You would do and when. All I knew is that there was quiet and it was freaking me out.

Maybe something could still be done. One look at what The Colors were doing re-affirmed that the group was truly dissolved.

Andrea, The Blue One, who was once considered a catalyst in his own right, the literary muse that would help build the framework for this story, had betrayed the group. More specifically he had burned me and spurned Fellini. With the publication of *Yucatan,* a mostly fictionalized version of our adventure together, he had made himself out to be a hero type, a frustrated adventurer trying to corral the crazy he was experiencing. He made my character look like a cheap used car salesman, a sexual predator, and the typical dumb blonde without even a hint of spirituality. He made Fellini look like a buffoon, an easily-led fool who also tried to manipulate others to get what he wanted. In the years following our trip to Tulum, both Fellini and I had helped Andrea in many ways. I actually housed and fed him while he was working on this manuscript, something that truly devastated me later. I knew he and I never really understood each other, but I didn't think he could be this cruel. Any chance we had at a relationship was crushed when he promised me a role in his film *Treno di Panna,* which he later gave to actress Carol Alt. I was done with The Blue One and so was Fellini...for good.

Sybil, the original White One, had been out of touch ever since she called us devil worshippers. I wouldn't see her for another twenty-five years when I ran into her at the Sundance Film Festival. At the time, hers was not an energy that was missed. Still, she was a missing piece of the original puzzle.

Maurizio, The Yellow One, had also gone. He continued working with his father Alberto on films, including one final one with Fellini, *Ginger and Fred*. There were still bad feelings about the trip as Maurizio spent a lot of his father's money in what was supposed to be pre-production for a Castaneda film and it never materialized into anything. In fact, Alberto financed *Ginger and Fred* partially because he thought the Castaneda film would eventually come together afterward. When Fellini moved on to *Intervista,* that essentially severed that working relationship and our contact with The Yellow One as well.

Brinke, the other Violet One, only received one phone call, as I mentioned. I am still in contact with Brinke, though she wasn't in touch with The Voice, after I moved to Rome, but it made an impression she will never forget. Her being my roommate was an adventure in itself. There was The Orange One, whose participation was short-lived. The Grey One also came and went. We never saw either of them again.

There was also the new White One, Philipo. I could never quite get a read on him. He was trying to be a personal tarot reader to Fellini as well and was extremely possessive of him. He said he had heard The Voice a few times and that was it. He was never really interested in pursuing things further and he bristled at any mention of it as he knew it would take away from Fellini's focus on him.

The only one who was still involved in pursuing it was Tullio. After he heard from The Voice, he seemed to understand its importance. Tullio was the only one other than me that actively pushed Fellini to make this film, to acquiesce to The Voice, and understand the importance of it all. He was a crucial partner when Fellini tired of hearing my own pleas. I wasn't privy to many of their conversations, but I know Tullio was regularly in contact with both You and Fellini and was trying, like myself, to get them on the same page...even after Fellini told him to back off.

That was all that was left. Me, Tullio and Fellini, who fought tooth and nail against The Voice every step of the way. We also occasionally had support from Vincenzo and Milo, though they never received calls. This was a far cry from what You had envisioned, I'm sure. This was a far cry from the unit that was supposed to deliver a message that would change the world. I struggled with those feelings of failure for not keeping everyone together, though I knew better. I knew the group had always been fragmented and were never going to be the spiritual force You had hoped for and envisioned. That aspect of the mission was simply never going to happen, not with this group, despite my best efforts, which I admittedly hadn't given in years.

I wondered if anything could be salvaged. I had a partner in Tullio and there was always Fellini's curiosity. Despite his frustrations and his desire to be done with The Voice, he was still intrigued by what was out there, why they had reached out and what it all meant.

Then, finally, inexplicably, he decided he was going to explore it.

It was completely out of the blue.

When he announced that his next project would be *The Voice of the Moon*, I was shocked. I was certain he was finally going to do it. He was finally going to listen to You and try to address what they wanted of him. He was going to show off our experience and even more important, he was going to try and show some of what we learned, a peek at what had happened and why. He was going to bring You's message to the masses…

…sort of.

With Fellini, nothing was so simple. *The Voice of the Moon*, what would be his final masterpiece, was no different. It was his own. It was nobody else's. It was complex, beautiful, confusing, tragic, personal, and universal. It was the compromise between what he wanted and what You wanted. It was a mystery. It was pure Fellini.

Chapter 24

La Voce della Luna

La Voce della Luna was the closest we were going to get to any sense of finality to our story. It was the result of first mystery, intrigue, and drama and then later, years of physical and psychological torment to a genius of man who was always handling the demons that watch over our great artists. It was the result of those closest to him, who knew Fellini intimately and knew of his adventure in the jungles of Mexico constantly pushing and urging him to serve not just his greater purpose, but a universal mission, to use his art to truly open up the eyes of humanity to the possibilities of something else, something more, something spectacular. It was the result of fatigue, hope, need, desire, strain, stress, ego. While he would only hint at its true intention, even to those of us closest to him, we all knew *La Voce della Luna* was done for The Voice. It was You's film…done how Fellini wanted to do it.

Finally.

To try and completely understand the plot and themes of *La Voce della Luna,* or any Fellini movie in any sense of rationality or detail is a practice in frustration and borderline insanity. There is too much to absorb in the tapestry of his moving art. Too much happens and it happens quickly. Fellini never hesitated with any of his films to switch the pace and the story at the drop of a dime, following his artistic instincts and the calling of the muse rather than the trivialities of plot device and structure. This would come to define him and he carried his particular chaotic style, fueled by his ego and genius, all the way through to the end of his career. Say what you will about the scope of Fellini's films and when and where he peaked, but no critic or casual film fan could ever say Fellini compromised or changed for anyone. From his first to his last, and everything in between, they were all Fellini films and *only* Fellini films.

The beauty was and still is, all these years later, in the insanity.

With *La Voce della Luna,* there was an extra bit of crazy…and I'm not talking about the infusion of our story. I'm talking literal crazy.

There was no way Fellini was going to simply share our tale as it happened. He had proven his stubbornness and defiance many, many times over the past five plus years. The closest he would ever get was *Trip to Tulum* and even the graphic novel took too many liberties, at least in the eyes and ears of The Voice. Now, even though he was trying again, the story itself wouldn't suffice, not to Fellini. Whether it was out of comfort, pride, or purely creative license, Fellini needed something more for this film, some other way to present what he wanted to say.

La Voce della Luna was partially based on and inspired by the critically acclaimed book *Il Poema dei Lunatici* by Ermanno Cavazzoni. "Poems of the lunatics." That was the base from which Fellini would construct his final monument to the insanity of life itself. As surprised as we all were that Fellini would choose this as his source material, in a way, it made sense. First of all, it gave him the distance he needed to feel safe in telling the tale. Plus, at many times during our adventure and the years that followed, we all felt like we were going a little insane. Too many things happened that we simply couldn't comprehend, that our rational minds couldn't come to terms with and it took its toll. We tried as best as we could, but whenever The Voice called, we felt our minds slipping. It was our difficult, deranged secret and we had nobody to share it with. Because of that, because of what we experienced, we were now all lunatics in our own right. The Voice had made us as such. In a sense, it was a perfect blanket with which to cover our own tale.

The film itself, like all Fellini films, is open to interpretation, but there is an undeniable personal, philosophical approach to the quest for the meaning of life that is present throughout. It definitely deals with elements of nature and the supernatural as well as harmony and communion. There is a sense given in the film that there is so much more to hear if we would just listen, so in that sense, it addresses issues of communication and higher powers. There are also Fellini's jabs at societal problems, a trademark of his later career films. There are glimpses of his thoughts on aristocracy, technology, the classes, and the ever-changing hearts, minds, and souls of humanity. And of course, *La Voce della Luna* examines the limits of the human psyche, what pushes it, and how far it can bend before it tragically and dramatically breaks.

The "plot" is relatively simple: A vagabond and a former politician wander together through the Italian countryside finding themselves in a small city preparing for a garish festival, encountering colorful characters and a number of chaotic situations, including television commercial productions, a beauty pageant, a twisted disco, rock concerts, and religious rituals and celebrations.

To add to the stark nature of this incredibly deep, sad, and dramatic film, Fellini surprised everyone by casting many famous comedic Italian actors, including Roberto Benigni and Paolo Villaggio, among others. Benigni plays the vagabond who hears voices telling him how to change the world and Villaggio is the politician who becomes convinced through his paranoia that people are merely puppets playing roles in a bigger plan. These two characters, more than anything else in the film, reflected Fellini's feelings about our experience together, the constant influence of The Voice and the meaning of it all. Like Fellini himself during our adventures, both of these characters are often confused, but ever moving forward.

The film also deals with the characters first hearing whispers from the moon and then their efforts to capture it, lasso it down, and the violent, disturbing chaos that ensues when representatives from different aspects of society come together to celebrate its capture.

Is that what we were trying to do? Did Fellini feel like this is how society would react to You's message? It was a depressing thought, but I wasn't sure he was wrong. If we truly fulfilled You's plan for us, if we played according to their rules and offered up their message, maybe chaos would break out. Maybe we as a civilization weren't ready. Maybe that was Fellini's worry all along. I know from our talks that he had deep concerns about the state of our world and the disservice we do to each other as we all focus on our own individual goals and ideologies. While he could often find beauty in the world, Fellini also saw the darker side and it concerned him. That's why he so often went to the mystic forces of the I Ching and the tarot in a constant search for answers. Anybody who watched his movies could see that he celebrated both sides, the mystical and the banal equally, acknowledging that the dark and the light were in a constant fight for power, always looking to tip the balance.

Fellini never really talked about the themes or the inspiration for his films, even with those to which he was closest. I gathered from my many conversations with him that it was difficult for him to explain exactly when and where the muse hit him and why it wanted to show itself in any particular way. It was also partially the reason he rarely worked from a fully fleshed out script. Fellini's inspiration was fluid, always changing. He might wake up with an idea in the morning and trash it by night, completely changing key moments in his film as he followed an artistic whim. He was also, as I mentioned, one to never look back.

We talked a lot on this project as I became intimately involved with the production, but Fellini remained closed off on certain points, even to me. He wasn't interested in explaining why he was making this film or why now. He wouldn't discuss what was happening or what things meant. He was silently going about his job, balancing the light and the dark in himself...his desires and those of The Voice. If I had any doubts about Fellini's intentions, even with all his imagery and the defining characteristics of his two heroes, they were satisfied with the last line of *La Voce della Luna*.

"If we all quieted down a little, maybe we'd understand something."

He gave other glimpses as well, even some in public. In an interview, Fellini admitted that he was constantly haunted by vengeful spirits or other creatures who he believed he had angered over the last few years. He said they were constantly toying with him and he hoped this film would help silence them because he was tired.

"I get exhausted when I'm trying any way I can to put off starting a film. It's an honest to goodness matter of a starting neurosis, this attitude of total aversion like someone who puts off the moment when he'll have to look at himself in the mirror, an image he wants to disown. It's worsened in these last years," he said. "I have a tendency to hold off starting a film until I feel myself forced to begin in order to see where I want to go, where I will take myself…I covered this last film with insults, I tried to kick it away like one does with an illness you don't want to catch. In order not to catch pneumonia, what do you do? You try to defend yourself."

But eventually, he said, he knew it had to be made.

The way he finally relented, finally adhered to You's demands is actually rather genius in itself. Fellini was able to frame The Voice as something coming from an entire cast of crazy people. Through the source material and his main characters, Fellini was able to protect himself from both judgement and the personalization of the story he so desperately wanted to avoid. His idea was that if people thought hearing a mysterious alien voice was insane, he could hide behind the fact that his characters were in fact, insane. It allowed him to safely tell our story in the medium You wanted while also keeping himself slightly removed, thus satisfying his needs and desires.

When I heard about his desire to make the film, I was stunned. It was a short, simple conversation with Fellini, but one I'll always remember. He called me in to throw the coins with him, saying he wanted an early reading on a new project. When I asked what the project was, his voice was strong and definitive.

"I'm going to talk about The Voice."

That was it. After all this time, he made the decision on his own and he made it sound like it wasn't any kind of big deal. I had pushed him for years as had Tullio and others. We were always met with denial, frustration, anger or worse, silence.

"What made you change your mind?"

"It's time," he replied, urging me to get the coins ready for his reading. It was clear he didn't want to talk details. But I had one more question.

"How are you going to tell it?"

Federico furrowed his brow and grimaced. He simply didn't like talking about process with anyone, especially in this case. He was still clearly not comfortable with any of this and he never would be.

"Christina, I don't know. Maybe you can tell me," he said as he pointed to the coins.

From that moment on, it was purely the business of making the film, one that would prove in its own right, to be a fitting end to an amazing legacy, one that would help him fulfill a greater purpose that divine beings intended for him.

During this entire process, The Voice would remain silent for both of us. I found that extremely weird, especially as we set forth on this particular adventure, but I assumed they were giving us space to finish what was started in 1984.

Finally, Fellini was going to finish the work. I would be there alongside.

Chapter 25

VERSO LA LUNA CON FELLINI

Fellini started shooting his final film in October 1989, and it would prove to be one of the longer shoots of Fellini's career. Almost right away, the rumors began that Fellini wasn't sure what he was doing with this film. He didn't have a clear idea and was improvising as he went. He had always directed that way to a certain extent, letting the muses speak to him rather than adhering to a specific course of action. But this was different. Actors, crew, writers all seemed lost as to what Fellini wanted and how they were supposed to help him fulfill his vision. There was frustration, anger, sadness, but mainly confusion…and this was within the first few weeks.

There was also beauty.

This was, after all, still a Fellini film and nobody could deny that the imagery he brought to his work was anything short of breathtaking. Deciphering his visions was often tricky, even for Fellini himself, but in the rare moments when everyone could get on the same page, those were the moments that bled beauty and excellence straight from Fellini's heart and soul.

I saw all of this happen, the chaotic roller coaster process of the making of Fellini's final film, up close and personal.

Since our adventures began, I was now a staple of Fellini's films, both on and off camera. However, he never really gave me any type of major role, or even supporting for that matter. He often used me as a featured extra at best, walking through a scene, acting sexy or simply just being the exotic blonde American standing in the corner. These were not dream roles and I often wondered why Fellini, who was very supportive of my career endeavors, never offered me something more. Over the years, I began to think it was because he didn't want me distracted. He liked having me as a spiritual counselor at his beck and call.

However, this time was different. This time I would be a lot more involved. I think one reason was that I was present for so much of the source material of this film. If Fellini was truly going to address our adventure together, then he knew I should be a part of it.

The other reason is because I asked.

Eugenio and I came up with an idea to film the process of making *La Voce della Luna*. We wanted to offer a real behind-the-scenes look at the great director in action, tackling a deeply personal project. We wanted something nobody had ever seen before—full access to the process and the players involved. Eugenio would direct and I would star in it as an American reporter there to watch il Maestro in action. We would show and tell the story, give the world an in-depth exploration of what it was like to work with one of the greatest directors of all time.

"Yes, you can do that, but work around me," Fellini said. "Don't bother me."

That was as close to an open welcome as we were going to get. We both knew he was acerbic about his process, surly about intrusions. We also both knew he had never agreed to anything like this before. The idea of making it the subject of a documentary was something I thought I would never see. We accepted his terms, knowing we had gotten something that others had only dreamed of and that we now had a chance to make a serious mark in the filmmaking world ourselves.

I think it felt good for Fellini; he felt like it was something he could offer to two people he loved. For me, I was very happy to include Eugenio in on my relationship with Fellini. Our marriage was definitely going through a rough patch and there were still feelings of deep jealousy about mine and Fellini's unique relationship. Now he could be involved and could see firsthand what it was and what it wasn't. I think it was also good for Fellini in that his wife Giulietta could also see that the known Lothario had absolutely nothing sexual happening with me! It would be a good arrangement for everyone.

As Fellini began work on his project, we began filming *Verso la Luna con Fellini* or, as it would become more commonly known once it started appearing on Italian television and later at film festival, *Towards the Moon with Fellini.*

Making that documentary was one of the hardest times in my life. It would be a nine-month shoot for Fellini and we were there the entire time. We were the first to arrive in the morning and the last ones to leave at the end of the day. We worked eighteen plus hours a day, often sleeping in the car and eating whatever was leftover from catering for Fellini's cast and crew. We were given little to no money by the film's producer. If I remember correctly, our entire documentary was made for under $10,000, a pittance that meant no money left over for us to cover even our most basic needs. It was a passion project and one that we marched on with night and day. We felt we were doing something new and important and that was worth the toll it was taking on us, including the twenty-five pounds I would lose during filming. If you watch the documentary closely, you can see me shrink as it goes on.

Our film uses the framework of a ragtag documentary team on a quest, seeking to find Fellini and then running into him as he begins work on his next film and an even greater mission…searching for the voice of the moon. He allows us to come along for the ride, and we watch the constant struggle of the genius and the troubled artist as he tries to both appease and silence *The Voice* by tight-roping on the brink of beauty and madness.

In the film, we see flashes of his multiple personalities. We see him woo and enchant the people he works with one minute and then berating them the next. We see his anger and frustration as well as his charm and passion. We hear yelling one minute and we see smiles the next. Mostly, though, we see a conflicted director trying desperately to get what he wants from his cast and crew without really even knowing himself what it is and how it can be executed. We see him following actors around with his bullhorn, shouting out commands. We see him dousing an actress with flour because he felt the makeup was applied wrong. We see him literally positioning actors and their limbs to make a shot look exactly as he likes. We see him applying graffiti to a wall to get a scene looking exactly as he likes. We see everyone watching him in awe and wonder every step of the way.

Despite their apparent frustrations, it's still a lovefest for cast and crew. In the documentary, I turn to them often to ask about Fellini and the process, focusing mainly on the two stars Benigni and Villaggio as well as the producers. No one can really tell me anything about the film they're working on. None of them have seen a script or received any instructions from the great director on what they're supposed to do. Everyone feels as though they're being kept in the dark. Yet they show up, hoping to learn more and help fulfill his vision each and every day.

You can see their devotion. Like the actors, writers, producers and crew that have come before them, they are willing to follow Fellini. The lack of a plan does not deter them. They trust in him and he rewards them with moments of brilliance. They know that they are working on a Fellini film and that in itself is important. As Benigni says in the documentary, "All films by Fellini are love stories and all love stories are Fellini films."

The one thing they all have in common on this project, from Fellini on down…is they believe they are being guided by the moon.

"Doing a film is like taking a trip to the moon," says one of the producers. To be fair, it's what this felt like. I don't know if it was the subject matter, the exhaustion or the influence of Fellini himself, but we all bought into the idea that we working under universal guidance. It made sense for Fellini and I, after all we had experienced. But we weren't alone. Every single person who worked on *La Voce della Luna* worshipped the moon during that process, letting it guide us every step of the way.

"I often hear the moon talking and she says shocking things I cannot repeat to you," Benigni says. "I found the sun to be mute while the moon spoke. The stars were particularly raspy. The moon, she has a very special voice and from her voice, we got the idea for this film."

That was truer than he could ever know.

And yet…something bothered me. Something bothered me greatly. Two things actually.

One, as this process went on and I saw what Fellini was filming, I realized it had very little, if anything, to do with our actual adventure. I felt it had even less to do with what The Voice wanted us to do. Other than the idea of voices coming from the universe, there were no other similarities. Even with my vast knowledge of Fellini's reliance on symbols, I still couldn't decipher anything, veiled or otherwise, that would reflect what we had experienced or what we were supposed to say. Again, I wasn't even sure what we *were* supposed to say but I knew this wasn't it. It almost felt as if Fellini had started with the idea of possibly tackling You's mission for us, but his fears, ego, and perhaps even confusion about the whole thing, pushed him further and further away as the process went on. Since he didn't have a solid plan going into it, the process itself diverted him from fulfilling You's purpose. Fellini always went where his inspiration took him and if that meant going off course and getting away from The Voice's requests, commands, demands, whatever, then so be it.

This was not going to be the movie I thought it would be, no matter how it turned out.

The second thing is that throughout the entire process, The Voice was silent. Neither of us heard from them. Not one call. Not one sign.

That terrified me.

Chapter 26

Silence and Catharsis

"I have these dreams where I am floating aimlessly at sea. I am stuck in this boat and I feel everything slipping away. They are clearer now. They are more vibrant. They are more real. I do not know what it means, but Christina, I am so scared."

Fellini was exhausted. He wrapped shooting *La Voce della Luna* in June of 1990 and the entire process had completely wiped him out. He was the most vulnerable I had ever seen him, a surprising state of being for such a powerful man I was used to seeing in control. He was truly lost and I suddenly saw his age, his experience and, dare I say, how much closer he was to the end of it all.

"I also dream that I am walking the streets of my hometown and there is no home. There is nothing. I do not exist there."

These were daily conversations I was now having with Federico. He felt more and more compelled to share each and every mood, fear, emotion, dream. We studied books about dreams together, read tarot, and tossed the coins multiple times a day now. Fellini asked questions about everything, including this most recent project. The answers were more and more convoluted, unclear as to what things meant and where things were going. For as much as we worked on our documentary, Fellini had poured his heart and soul into this project as well. Fellini seemed lost because he *was* lost and wrapping up the project hadn't brought him the same catharsis that his other projects often did. Rather, it just brought him more questions and fears. It brought him doubts and troubles.

That, in turn, brought him closer to me. In times of trouble, Fellini clung to those he needed most and I was one of the few on the top of that list. I did like the fact that he needed me and that I could be there to help him. But I also saw just how much this was affecting him and it made me feel rather helpless at times. All I could do was be with him as a friend, a spiritual guide, and a partner who understood at least a fraction of what he was going through.

However, I had no real answers.

As the movie wrapped and was put into the hands of the producers and distributors, all we could do was wait to see how it would be received. There would be a slight delay and that always affected Fellini, especially later in his career. He prided himself pretending to not care about what people thought. But, at his heart, he was an emotional artist and one who craved approval. With the long string of critical flops he experienced toward the end of his career, that need grew. It got harder and harder for Fellini to wait and see how the public, the critics, his peers, everyone would react to his latest offering, the latest baring of his soul.

As we waited for the film to make its debut, Federico would constantly ask me what I thought of the work. It was hard for me to answer. I still wasn't sure, even after the countless hours spent watching him work, exactly what kind of film Fellini had made or even what it was about. I would be willing to bet that if anyone asked any participant in that project, they would answer the same. Still, he was my mentor, friend, and spiritual adventurer, and I didn't want to do anything to add to his ever-increasing fears.

I had a fear of my own…silence. I could understand why You wasn't present during the filming itself. First of all, we were working so hard and we were not actually physically near a telephone very often. Mercifully, this happened before the prominence of cellphones, and we weren't as easily accessible as we are now. Second, I always felt they were giving Fellini the space to figure it out as he went. I felt these evolved beings would, in a sense, respect the process and give him the opportunity to work it out in his way. You, like the rest of us, was also waiting to see what Fellini would do.

But now, shooting was done and we spent a lot of time sitting in offices waiting. There was plenty of opportunities to hear from them and yet, nothing.

What did that mean?

I had a sinking suspicion that You was not pleased.   I feared that they were angry and I waited to see what that meant. I wondered what they would do.

Meanwhile, I experienced two amazing things in the times before *La Voce della Luna* made its debut.

First, we wrapped our documentary *Towards the Moon with Fellini* and we were all very pleased with how it turned out. For as much blood, sweat, and tears that we poured into it, we had something that nobody had ever done before; a very intimate look at one of the most legendary directors at work. It was a study in a tumultuous yet sacred process. There was a reviewer of the documentary that later put it perfectly.

"*Towards the Moon* is rewarding for anyone who has ever loved a Fellini film. Here he is in all his glory, a warm, patrician presence thriving amid a constant swirl of activity and throngs of people, knowing what he wants and how to get it while one suspects no one else really knows what's going on…By the time *Towards the Moon* is over, it leaves the viewer with an inevitably poignant sense of loss—of Fellini's love of humanity even more than his great gift at expressing it."

We had captured something magical, even before we all knew that we had filmed him shooting his last masterpiece. We were able to see and then share Fellini's devotion to his visions and his need to express his thoughts, feelings, and passions to anyone willing to watch. Fellini always had a message, even if he didn't quite know what it was, and he wanted everyone to know. I believe that's the true reason You had found and chosen him. We had caught him in the act of forming that message as best he could.

On a personal level, I was very excited. The documentary came out on Italian television as part of a special right before the movie was released and it was wildly successful. The people of Italy loved getting this up close and personal look at one of their most celebrated native sons. They called the documentary "funny," "sweet," "beautiful." It helped build a great buzz for Fellini's film and I truly thought that if *La Voce della Luna* was successful, this documentary could be mine and Eugenio's big break.

The second thing that happened to me was a true lesson in catharsis and one I soon discovered I really needed as it brought me some closure and an awareness as to where I was and who I had become.

I was sitting in Fellini's office one day after having just given him a reading when his phone rang.

"Christina, can you get that?" Fellini yelled from the other room. This was very strange as I rarely took his calls for him. I'll be honest, for a split second, I wondered if I wasn't going to hear that all-too-familiar crackle as soon as I put the phone to my ear.

Instead, I heard a voice from my past, one I recognized instantly. It was my old flame, the famous director I had dated in my youth, the one that proved to be part of the catalyst for my moving away from New York.

Woody.

I hadn't thought about him in years, though his effect on me was still a major presence in my life, especially when it came to relationships.

"Pronto, one moment please," I stuttered into the phone after he asked to speak with Fellini. I turned to Fellini and explained who it was with a look of shock on my face. Fellini knew about my past. We had talked exhaustively about that relationship many times and how it had affected me.

"What does he want?" Fellini asked sharply.

"Well, he wants to talk to you."

With a crisp wave of his hand, Fellini let me know that he didn't want to be bothered.

"I am so sorry, but Mr. Fellini cannot come to the phone," I said. Then, on impulse, I fessed up. "I think I ought to let you know this is Babi Christina Engelhardt. I send my best regards."

"What happened to you?! You just disappeared from my life!" I heard instant surprise and excitement coming from the other end of the phone and I could tell it was genuine. I wasn't sure what I had expected, but it certainly wasn't this level of happiness!

I told Woody I was living in Italy and working for Fellini.

"Wow, that is just great. I admire him so much. My agent gave me his number and I thought to call." Then he paused and his voice got softer and gentler. "I was worried I lost you, but for you to leave me for Fellini…well, I am okay that you left me for someone I admire."

He laughed and I laughed along with him, letting years of bitterness finally roll off my shoulders. I could feel an actual weight being hoisted, disappearing forever. I hadn't realized how much I had still harbored feelings of hurt, anger, and confusion from this life-changing relationship. Getting this closure was helping me put it all in perspective and, even more important, move on.

"I wish you the best," he said and with that, we hung up. It was a very strange moment for me. Years later, when I sent him a copy of my documentary, he wrote back to me with the nicest letter, acknowledging me with fondness. It meant the world to me to have that cleared up. It was an emotional healing and it uplifted my feelings towards one of the two men who have influenced me the most in my life. This was a phone call I would not forget. More than anything, it made me appreciate even more the opportunity to be by Fellini's side.

As the movie got ready for its release, that would be exactly where he needed me to be once again.

Chapter 27

JOIN US, LEAD US, LEAVE IT ALL BEHIND

But first, we experienced a little diversion that was both extremely bizarre and terrifying in its own right. I guess you could call it my "missed opportunity" at becoming a full-fledged cult leader.

"Christina, you need to come to my office at once," Fellini said over the phone and I could hear a mixture of fear and amusement in his voice. "There are some people who want to meet you. They have something very important that they want to ask us."

What the hell could this possibly be? As we still waited for *La Voce della Luna* to be released and we watched with eager anticipation and joy as our film made an impact with Italian audiences, my mind began racing as to potential opportunities. I was excited by this phone call. Maybe this was more work, another opportunity for Eugenio and myself to handle another project. There were endless possibilities and I was thrilled by them all.

Except for what it ended up being.

I walked into Fellini's office to see him sitting with four men and two women, all dressed like business professionals ready for another day at the office. They sat stoic, waiting for my arrival.

Were these producers? Lawyers? What?

As I entered, Fellini greeted me with a hug and a smile, but I could tell there was also a look of veiled confusion and concern on his face and that worried me. I turned to the group of strangers, put on a smile and simply said, "Hello."

They greeted me with smiles of their own, though they seemed rather forced, almost...robotic. That in itself led me to a moment of great panic.

"Is this You?!" I thought to myself. "Have they taken a human form so they could come talk to us? Oh my God, they're not happy with our work, with our failure as the group of colors! They've come here to punish us! This is what I feared! How do we save ourselves?! What can we do?!"

Those fears quickly dissipated and utter confusion set in as soon as the group's spokesperson greeted me.

"Hello Christina, we are the followers of Carlos Castaneda. We have traveled a long way to meet with you. We know all about you and your work with Mr. Fellini. We also know that you are devout followers of the teachings of Don Juan. We come to you with a great question, a blessed mission and opportunity. We come to both of you with a calling. Our great teacher is moving on. It is time for our group to seek new "seers." We are searching for those worthy to lead us in our great cause. We are looking for the enlightened souls that will continue the good work and show us the true way. We want you and Mr. Fellini to join us and lead us."

What the fuck?! Is this for real?!

Let me first add a little context. We hadn't heard from Castaneda or really anything about him. We still admired the teachings of Don Juan, but even those had lost their luster after our experience with the work's author. To be completely blunt, we had written Castaneda and his followers off as nothing more than a confused cult being led by a clueless, overwhelmed, manipulative egotist. Once You started becoming more of a presence in our lives, we literally moved on to bigger things.

Over these six-plus years, however, Castaneda and his followers had gone through changes of their own. Whereas people around the world were once fascinated by his teachings and the brilliance of his writing, now he had developed the reputation of a troubled recluse and a slick illusionist…some even calling him a fraud. They questioned the existence of Don Juan, the great shaman Castaneda supposedly met at a Greyhound station in Arizona who then led him into his journey of transformation and growth, sharing his ancient wisdom. Others asked whether or not Castaneda was a true channel for him and if so, why. His teachings were now openly debated. Despite the fact that his brilliantly-written books sold over eight million copies, the legitimacy of the work was now being called into question. Castaneda had emerged for a brief time to once again make public appearances to teach his Tensegrity. However, by all accounts, this criticism had pushed him deeper into seclusion and even more erratic behavior.

He also began surrounding himself with even stranger followers—witches, drug addicts, even diehard fans that could be considered stalkers. Of course, a majority of his followers, at least those who lived with him, were women and they were all allegedly his lovers. These women made the news as many of them cut off ties with their former lives when they took residence with Carlos. They shut off communication with friends and family and in many cases, took new names. In more recent years, there have been published accounts by former followers who talk of simply bizarre demands from Carlos to help them become more devout or separate from their pasts or in some cases, simply to show loyalty and devotion. Followers were scolded for trying to figure out where they were when taken to the jungles. They were given random jobs, one even told to work part time at a McDonalds for some reason. Pets were to be released or destroyed. Hugs or other signs of affection were not permitted with others. Carlos allegedly made some new devotees get in contact with their families one last time to actually damn them to hell. Many said later they felt like they were being held prisoner. Even those that loved him lived in fear as he would dismiss followers with the snap of a finger. As one former devotee described, they never knew where they stood. Some lasted mere hours in the compound while others would be there for years only to be dismissed because of something as trivial as drinking too much coffee. He also famously lambasted having children, yet hid a son for many years. It was one more piece of hypocrisy. What actually happened deep in the jungles of Tulum is of course up for debate, but there have been enough accounts to know that whatever it was, it was disturbing to say the least.

This would last all the way up to Carlos's death in 1998 and what happened to many of these women remains a deep mystery. Many of them disappeared forever, not even re-surfacing after Carlos's death. In at least one case, a follower's skeleton was discovered years later in the middle of Death Valley. Now, a lot of this happened after this meeting with Fellini and me, but even then, the rumors of more and more erratic behavior by Carlos and his people were leading some to question the sanity of Don Juan's followers.

Now here they were in Fellini's office, asking us to lead.

"But what about Carlos?" was all I could ask, clearly flummoxed by the entire experience. I could never get a clear response. What I gathered was that Carlos was either sick or possibly even dead, but they wouldn't answer delusional for even his own followers and he was losing their loyalty. My thought now was that they were looking for new leadership to maintain what they had built. Castaneda was no longer showing them the way and, like his devotees, he too was dispensable.

Of the six, only one person spoke. He was clearly the group's leader.

"You are to be the new seers. We need a male and a female and it is clearly you two."

Fellini remained silent, sitting and taking it all in with no expression on his face. I waited for him to ask the obvious question, but it was clear he wouldn't. So it was up to me.

"Why us?" I asked almost dreading the answer. He went on to describe newspaper articles where we hinted at out meeting with Carlos and our old devotion to the teachings of Don Juan, the work we did with *Trip to Tulum,* accounts from *Yucatan* and even more recently what they had seen in the *Towards the Moon with Fellini* documentary.

"It is obviously you two."

We sat in silence for a moment, not sure what to make of all this.

"You must come with us right now. You will live with us in the compound in Mexico. You must leave immediately and not tell anyone where you are going or why. You are disciples already and now it is your turn to lead. Come join us. Lead us."

Again, there was silence and my head was reeling. I was too stunned to even respond. I couldn't believe this was real. One thing I was absolutely sure of…there was no way I was going to leave with them. There was no way I was going to drop everything and move to the jungles of Tulum. The idea of leaving my husband, my family, everyone was terrifying. There was no way I was going to go with them.

But what if Fellini wanted to? What then? Would he see this as a calling? As the next great adventure? He had been tired and feeling the pressures of his life and career lately and this kind of move was certainly not outside the realm of possibilities for him, was it? Would he be willing to just pick up and leave forever? Could he disappear?

"Well, we thank you for your interest but there is absolutely no way we are doing that so thank you and goodbye."

Oh thank God!

For the next several minutes, the group just stood there, absolutely stunned at our refusal. They tried to convince us of our destiny, of our calling to lead. They were met with silence by me and increasing anger by Fellini, who eventually convinced them, angrily, to leave and to not contact us again.

Once they were gone, Fellini and I sat and simply looked at each other. Then we both shared a hearty laugh, thinking of the possibility of he and I leading a group of religious followers. It was truly one of the more bizarre experiences of my crazy, chaotic life.

Unfortunately, Castaneda's followers didn't give up without a fight. Fellini and I were both followed and approached for months.

At home, work, the supermarket, the park, wherever, we would run into them and when confronted, they would once again plea with us to reconsider. It was actually a terrifying few months with varying levels of aggression from them. Some would simply observe. Others would try to befriend me, telling me they were my shadow. Others acted more aggressively, demanding I go with them.

It would eventually let up as they soon began to realize that we were not the leaders they had in mind and they moved on to other targets, thus capping my missed chance at guiding my own people, becoming a spiritual guru and rising to the ranks of cult leader.

With Federico Fellini.

As if communicating with aliens wasn't enough!

Life can truly be bizarre at times.

Chapter 28

FELLINI'S LOST AND LAST FILM

La Voce della Luna was going to be Fellini's triumphant return. It was going to push him back to the elite status he created, that he defined for not just Italian cinema but for the art as a whole. It was going to spread You's message, unite people, make everyone look to and for something more. On a purely selfish level, it was going to propel us and the documentary into an even more successful career in film and television. Mainly, it was going to be the culmination of our long journey together, an expression of the beauty and the madness we had experienced for over seven years and what it all meant. *La Voce della Luna* was going to change things.

Unfortunately, it got panned and soon after, canned.

In the world of cinema, there is only one true power. Regardless of where your film comes from, how it was inspired and what it's trying so desperately to say, only a few voices truly matter. Love, honor, tragedy, heartbreak, friendship, unity, death—these themes all are relatively inconsequential in their importance compared to the defining force, the "gods" who rule what we see and don't see, what we experience and what we do not…the studios, the promoters, the critics.

Upon its release, *La Voce della Luna* was almost universally criticized among industry experts and the few fans that saw it. It received slightly positive reviews from some long-standing Fellini fans at first, which was more out of respect and loyalty than true reverence for the picture. But once it appeared at Cannes, where it was loathed, the floodgates opened. One respected critic absolutely doomed the film, saying he had "never been so bored in my life." Many film fans and even devout Fellini followers agreed, claiming they couldn't identify with the story, the characters, or the structure. It became the first Fellini film ever not to receive North American distribution. Also, it only showed for a few weeks in Italy, making it the shortest run of a Fellini film ever.

Being pulled from the shelves early may have contributed to the problem. In the past, Italian audiences had sometimes needed more time to warm up to Fellini's films. In fact, some of what are now considered his greatest films initially struggled at the box office. Fellini's style is enigmatic and often calls for multiple viewings, or at least time to process and to truly grasp what is happening. The mind needs time to take in all the subtle and expansive splendor. If you don't believe me, pick any of his films and watch it twice and see how much more you absorb on the second viewing. Audiences struggled to identify with *La Voce della Luna* and word spread quickly. Unfortunately, its stay in the theaters was so short that there was no chance for many people to see it themselves, or for those who did see it, to let it sink in or see it again, and the film suffered.

There are several reasons why critics took issue with the film. Many didn't like the seemingly improvised dialogue and action. The style of the film seemed jaded and sporadic, and the overuse of imagery and convoluted plot was a stretch even for the artistic nature of Fellini films. In many ways, some felt he had "over-Fellinied." Patrons grasped to make any sense of what was happening in the film or what anything meant. Plus, the movie featured some of Italy's greatest comedic actors and put them in ridiculously cynical and dour roles, back-dropped by sadly crazy people and circumstances. Quite simply, the film was too abstract and audiences could tell that Fellini himself was unsure of what he was doing with it.

I couldn't blame them. As filming went on and I realized that this film had nothing to do with You or our experience together, I too wavered back and forth on my thoughts on the quality of the project.

In watching Fellini so closely and working as his confidante, I could also tell he was challenged with this project and no esoteric advice could make an impact. He would ask the mystics for guidance, we would read the cards or throw the coins and I would tell him what they were saying…and then he would ignore the readings and go off to do his own thing.

News of its failure didn't surprise me, though the short shelf life did.

Part of the reason for the short stay was definitely the critical fallout and the disappointment of the earlier screeners. However, the film also experienced tragedy in terms of its producers and an awkward transition that left it hanging in limbo.

The film's executive producer was an old friend of Fellini's, a renowned Italian producer by the name of Mario Cecchi Gori. Mario was a sweet, heavyset, cigar-smoking man who adored Fellini and was thrilled to be working with him for the first time. Mario had made his mark with films like *The Easy Life, I Mostri, Mediterraneo,* and *Il Postino.* This was a passion project for Mario and a safety net for Fellini, who had pretty much burned bridges with most other producers in Italy and even abroad. Unfortunately, toward the end of filming, Mario got very sick and was diagnosed with severe lung cancer. His health declined quickly and he had to remove himself from the project, turning the reins over to his son, Vittorio.

Vittorio would eventually go on to be an arguably successful producer in his own right, working on films like *Life is Beautiful.* He would prove to have his own style of business savvy that worked for him for a while…as long as he was staying out of trouble. Vittorio was a noted playboy and hardcore partier. Not shy from the limelight and the watchful eye or potential for scandal that comes with it, Vittorio rather embraced it. Over his career, there would be rumors of drinking and drug binges and several affairs. He would also be arrested twice for poor business practices and would eventually run his studio into financial ruin.

This is the man who was charged with handling the final piece of Fellini's legacy. In my documentary, there is a moment where I'm interviewing him and he says, "For the first time in my life, I don't know what I'm doing."

Wonderful.

It was the classic case of the spoiled playboy being handed the keys to the empire without fully understanding the responsibilities that come with it. He inherited not only a tremendous fortune, but also projects and a career that were overwhelming for where he was at in his own life. Vittorio didn't have the same respect for or relationship with Fellini that his father had and as such, he didn't have the same investment in seeing this project succeed. In fact, Vittorio wasn't shy about his obsession with American films and he instantly started looking at projects he could involve himself with overseas.

When *La Voce della Luna* got the initially poor reviews, he balked and yanked it from the shelves. I wasn't close to Vittorio so I'm not exactly sure of the reasoning, but some have said it was fear of a flop. Others have pointed to Vittorio's sights being set on America. Still others claimed it was a solid business strategy to give the film *cult* status. Instead of keeping the film out for an extended run that might garner even worse criticism than it had already received, he could shelve it and make it Fellini's "mystery" project. The tougher it was to see, the greater the chance it had at becoming something mystical. Suddenly, *La Voce della Luna* was elusive and rare and those are words we often equate with greatness. It didn't quite work out that way, but at the time, the strategy, if that was in fact what Vittorio was shooting for, was sound. Regardless, *La Voce della Luna* was to be an overall disaster, a sad final chapter in the career of a great innovator.

Fellini knew it was a flop and he was disappointed. We talked after the film came out and though he never said it directly, it was clear that he knew he should have made the *real* story. He knew he had failed You and, in a sense, our experience together by shying away from what really happened and trying to cloak it with a tale of crazy adventurers. Not only in the interests of truth, but also our tale would have made for a more thrilling, and perhaps more accessible film.

But I found something else concerning. My friend was looking tired and frail and he now continued his talk of lacking passion for filmmaking as a whole. He spoke more negatively about his existence, the state of the world and what else was out there. He was losing faith and his belief in the unknown. Some of that was even present in the film as these wanderers look for something mystical in the moon only to find out there is nothing there. It was all a big disappointment, a fruitless quest.

I think, in a way, Fellini knew the end was near.

But we still had some adventuring left to do.

Chapter 29

Is You Gone?

You was gone.

It would take some time for me to officially accept their absence. For several years, You had been a constant, terrifying but intriguing presence in my life. After spending the beginnings of our "relationship" begging for them to either show me more or leave me alone, I had now not only accepted their presence, but also relied on it at times. I know that might sound weird, given everything I've written, but there is always comfort in the familiar and The Voice had become familiar.

Not long after we finished shooting our documentary and *La Voce della Luna,* which ate up all of our time, Fellini and I had a chance to breathe and re-assess where we were and what we were doing. We were also positive that You would reach out in some way, shape or form. Surely they had an opinion on what we had just done, on the film, on what was next. You had an opinion about everything. This couldn't be the exception. Even with how far Fellini had strayed from the real story, it was still the closest he got to fulfilling their request. Certainly there must be an opinion on it, whatever it may be. There also had to be a next step, right? Something else we were going to do?

Silence.

Looking back, I don't think I was as surprised that they didn't reach out. Communication had slowed over the past couple years. After all, You had tried working with us for half a decade and got, in the big scheme of things, very little out of all The Colors. We had disappointed them, ignored them, frustrated them and often times showed them we weren't capable of doing what they wanted us to do as a collective unit. At some point, You was going to just move on.

Now it seemed like they had.

I realized that the last real communication I had with You was my wedding night when they gave Eugenio and me their special sign. That was the last direct contact and that really struck me. Wow, that was two years ago! Had I been that busy and blind? Had I really not noticed they were out of my life for that long? Had I forgotten?

The answer wasn't so simple. That might have been the last *direct* contact, but they were certainly not gone. I felt You's presence everywhere. I constantly felt watched and even judged. I felt scrutinized in every choice I made, every step I took. I also felt completely and totally under their power at all times. It wasn't like they were physically controlling me, but more like they could if they wanted. They had shown us several times in the past their ability to physically alter and affect our reality, on both a small and grand scale and that they weren't afraid to do so whenever they wanted. That's tough to live with, if I'm being completely honest…knowing your life is really out of your hands. Maybe it was that idea that I couldn't shake or maybe they were still watching. Either way, I still felt You's presence and I often wondered if they weren't still making that presence felt from time to time.

Fellini could not have been more relieved to stop getting the phone calls. He kept receiving them for a time after You stopped reaching out to me, which I thought was strange. I was, after all, a lot more open to them and their needs and wants than anyone else in the group. During the filming of *La Voce della Luna,* Fellini got focused and stopped talking to me about the calls. Knowing he was locked into his project, I didn't push the issue. Plus, I was busy with my own.

Then, one day not long after shooting, during a reading I was doing for him, he brought it up.

"Christina," he said, looking right at me. "I think You is gone."

He said it quietly, as if to keep them from hearing. I can't be sure, but I feel like when he said those words, we both looked to the skies and braced ourselves for some kind of response.

"I don't know if they're gone, but they've stopped calling me," I answered.

"Me too," he said and there was that relief in his voice. "I tell you they are gone."

To be completely truthful, Fellini hadn't dealt with their invasion into his life very well. True, he was forever curious and even slightly honored to be picked by You, but he could never get past how they communicated. He didn't want to be connected to the strings he was so used to pulling. I would equate it to his feelings on the Catholic Church. He loved the idea of the saints, these great beings that he could pray to and ask for guidance. But, in reality, he didn't like the church itself with its rules and demands and sacrifices. He felt the same way about You. He wanted the experience and the knowledge they could give us of what else was out there, but he didn't want to follow their commands or play by their rules. He also couldn't get behind something he didn't understand, and You never gave him enough to satisfy his curiosity. After a while, the curiosity gave way to annoyance and anger. Fellini was done with this adventure.

Plus, even if he didn't admit it, he knew he had failed them and that was difficult for him to grasp. Fellini hadn't failed often in his life. Yet, here was a potentially grand mission, something from beyond the stars, something so unbelievable it would take great care and finesse to accomplish. Fellini, along with all of us, had seemingly botched it up, despite our best (and not-so-best) efforts. He worried that he failed, that You was angry, that whatever they were, they would have vengeance of some kind. He worried what that might be, the price of failure.

If they were gone, he could finally be free.

"It is over, Christina."

I truly didn't know how I felt about that.

Could this really be it? I feel like I asked that question more than any other during this adventure. Why would they leave us now? Don't get me wrong, I too had some feelings of relief at the thought of them not calling or visiting me in my visions anymore. I was quite content to not have a mission that I didn't understand or "bosses" that couldn't explain why I was doing what I was doing. I was just fine not dealing with the constant frustrations and fear.

Yet, I now felt empty and completely unsatisfied. What, if anything, had we accomplished? I struggled to find a comforting answer to that and that feeling of failure was one I couldn't shake. The past half-decade had to be for something so what was it?

As I left Fellini's office, I looked up at the sky and simply muttered, "Where are you?"

I got no response. I didn't know if that was a good thing or a bad thing. I also didn't know if I really wanted them to respond in any way. After all, we had failed and they had shown that if there was one emotion they understood, it was anger.

In the events that followed in my life and in Fellini's over the next couple years, I wondered if we weren't seeing that anger.

Chapter 30

Living in Fear

I've experienced a few terrifying injuries in my lifetime.

When I was filming *Russicum,* where I played an assassin, I had to endure a grueling physical shoot with lots of different kinds of combat, including work with weapons training. In it, my character gets shot. In Hollywood, to make shooting deaths more realistic, special effects experts use something called "squibs," which are essentially little pockets of fake blood that are attached to a person's costume and can be controlled to blow up when necessary, thus creating the effect of a bullet hitting a human target. When done right, the effect looks amazing.

When shooting *Russicum,* the effects technicians were struggling with the squibs and couldn't get them to stay attached…so they superglued them to me. Yes, I had little packets that were designed to explode superglued to my body. Sure enough, when the director called, "Action!" and the shootout happened, the technician triggered the squibs and they exploded right on me, creating not just searing pain, but essentially holes in my body where the squibs were placed. It honestly felt like I was really being shot and I couldn't believe how much it hurt.

A few years later, I went skiing with some friends in Big Bear, California and decided to brave a triple black diamond mountain. That was not a good call. I fell and fell hard, not able to stop myself from tumbling a good portion of the way down the mountain. In the process, I managed to tear my knees and had to be lifted down the mountain. Due to some insurance issues, I mainly had to let them heal on their own which meant a few months of doing nothing but lying around and sometimes crawling to get what I needed around the house. It was long and painful, a drain on me physically and mentally.

But perhaps the worst injury/accident of my life came not long after we wrapped *La Voce della Luna,* at a time I was questioning the disappearance of The Voice and our failure to give You what they really wanted. I was now spending my days looking over what we had done and what we hadn't, trying to figure out where we went wrong and if there would be any consequences to our failure.

That would be a thought that would stick with me for some time, especially after this accident.

In December of 1990, I was filming a movie called *Demonia.* The film description reads as follows: "A Canadian archaeological team in Sicily accidentally unleashes vengeful ghosts of five demonic nuns who were murdered 500 years earlier and the ghosts now set out to kill the group and townspeople alike."

It was the last day of filming and we were on location in one of the more horrifying locations I've ever been in. We were in an ancient church in Sicily where dead bodies were dressed in their finest clothes and essentially hung from the walls and ceiling as part of the way these ancient civilizations would both revere and prepare those who had passed on for what was waiting for them on the other side. It is very macabre, not a place you'd want to spend too much time. I just finished a scene where I have to find the mangled bodies of my co-actors. Of course, I did a lot of screaming.

When the scene was over, I went back to my trailer and pulled some tarot cards, trying to shake off the creepy feeling from working among the dead. It was also my birthday and I had a laugh at how I was spending the day. What was funny is I hadn't read for myself in a long while. I read for everyone on the set, but had ignored myself. Something was telling me to read now, however. When I did, I saw that something was going to "turn everything upside down in my life."

That worried me.

With The Voice still looming in my conscious, I felt anything could happen. I wasn't sure what this meant, but I feared it would be something major that would not go well for me. I was already on edge. Now I had a dire premonition and I wondered if You wasn't going to finally make its presence felt once again.

While I was closing the deck, our driver called me and the other actors from the shoot to take us back to our hotel. The four of us hopped into the car with the driver and my thoughts were admittedly elsewhere. The driver handled the car like a maniac. I was upset and scared and yelling at him to slow down, especially once it began to rain.

"We're fine," he yelled at me in Italian and turned the radio up so he couldn't hear me.

You arrogant prick, I thought and decided to tell him so.

"Hey, listen—"

Just then, we took a turn and our driver lost control, flipping the car off the road and rolling it multiple times down a hill into an orchard of lemon trees that literally caught us in mid-air. We simply hung there for a moment, upside down with the engine still running and the roof pinning us flat.

What happened? Oh my God, am I alive? Are we all alive?

And then, right away, another thought came screaming into my head.

Did You do this?

I snapped into action, quickly realizing because of the grueling pain I felt all over my body, but especially in my head, that I was alive. I checked on everyone. The driver and actor in the front seat were out cold or possibly dead. Their faces were covered in blood and broken glass. The two actors next to me seemed to be alright; they were starting to moan and move about. But we are all covered in shattered glass and upside down. Since I was in the middle of the back seat, I could more easily slither to the front and turn off the engine. I then worked my way out the back rear window, which was now only inches wide, and the other two actors from the back followed.

We sat there for a moment outside, trying to assess what had happened and just how hurt we were…and what should be done about the driver and the other actor in the front seat. They were still out cold and we weren't even sure how we could get to them or if they were still alive. We were also seemingly in the middle of nowhere, so we weren't sure how we could get help.

Just then, a farmer came running to us from behind the trees with a hacksaw in his hand. I was still trying to process what was happening when he looked at me, very concerned. He grabbed a lemon from one of the trees and cut it in half, taking part of it and squeezing it onto my head, yelling "disinfectant" in Italian.

At this point, I had no idea that I had large shards of glass sticking out of my head.

The lemon juice shot a new kind of stinging pain through me, but it also snapped me to attention. The three of us followed the farmer to his house where we were going to call for help. Along the way, we passed his tool shed and there I saw a large painting of an angel helping two young children over a bridge.

That's when I started to cry.

As a spiritual person, I felt protected, as if an angel reached down and saved us that day. The driver and the other actor would turn out to be fine too, just dinged up and knocked out in the accident. I felt blessed by a greater power.

But I also felt fear. I couldn't help but think You might have had a part in this. From what I had seen, this was definitely something they could have done. I thought of that painting of the angel and remembered how thrilled I was when they first reached out, how I actually thought of them as a higher power trying to show us something more, trying to help us cross that bridge.

Now I wondered if they weren't trying to kill me.

Over the next year, as I experienced heartache after heartache, I would keep this thought with me, wondering fearfully if You wasn't really gone at all.

With Penny Marshall, Robert De Niro, Meir Tepper, Art Linson,
Isabella Goldsmith. Mexico Christmas Trip, 1993.

Chapter 31

New and Powerful Friends

As I come toward the end of this tale with Federico Fellini, it is hard to relive all the frustration, anger, hurt, and yes, tragedy I experienced. It was not how the story was supposed to end, but, then again, life never really allows you to write the story you want. Sometimes, we must drift from the outline and simply accept where the adventure takes us, hoping that it ties into our narrative and leads us eventually to where we want to go.

As I approached 1993, my final year with Fellini, *our* final year with Fellini, I could do nothing but remember what once was, and even more, what wasn't. I could only focus on the opportunities missed and the obstacles that were now before me, pulling me further from the magic that was once so present in our lives.

There was no Voice so there was no purpose. I didn't know what to do…and that was only where my problems began.

I continued working on my acting career, though opportunities were getting harder to come by. I filmed a movie called *La Riffa*, a melodramatic love story with an intriguing twist. It would be one of the last I would do for quite some time. A dream I had since high school was proving to slip further and further from my grasp, and that was difficult to accept. That same year, I had my skiing accident, my dog died suddenly, my grandmother, who was such a vital influence in my life, died of lung cancer despite never smoking, and my apartment was broken into. It was not a year to remember, though it would become one I would never forget.

Eugenio began work on a fictional novel. At first, I was happy for him that he found another creative outlet. Our lives together and the chaos of the relationship seemed to settle more when he was wrapped up in a project. When he finished, I eagerly read what he had written only to find it was about a man who kills his wife and chops her into little pieces, leaving her in a suitcase on the side of a road.

This was the last straw for me. The relationship was over.

Honestly, it wasn't because of the book. That was just the proverbial straw, as it were. Eugenio and I couldn't seem to go longer than an hour or two without arguing about something. Anything. Everything. How to make coffee. The taste of the pasta sauce. What we wanted to do for the day. It didn't matter. Whatever it was, we would fight about it. In his nastier moments, he would stress to me how much he would never want to have children with me and that he could guarantee me that as I got older, he would step outside the marriage. I was so depressed and so upset by the constant yelling. It just wasn't in my nature and now it was becoming my life. I was tired of the jealousy he had with mine and Fellini's relationship. I was exhausted by his skepticism at not just my beliefs, but also the tales of You. I was brokenhearted.

So I left. We separated and then divorced officially much later, thus closing that particular chapter in my life.

With us now separated, I tried to figure out where to go or what to do. I waited for a sign, not necessarily from The Voice but just from anything or anyone. Fellini was of little support at this point as he was still reeling and resting from the last project, trying to decide what to do next while wrestling with his own demons. I started to shift my eyes back to America, thinking how nice it might be to go home and regroup.

Then, a sign came. At least, at the time, I thought it was a sign. I was so desperate at that point, so who knows? While hanging out with one of my actor girlfriends, I had the good fortune to meet Robert De Niro as well as the producers Arnon Milchan (*Brazil, The War of the Roses, JFK, Natural Born Killers, Fight Club, 12 Years a Slave)* and Meir Teper (*What's Eating Gilbert Grape?, From Dusk Til Dawn).* We all became close friends and, of course, I offered up my tarot services, with which they were all fascinated. Soon, I was seeing them regularly, especially Meir.

In fact, I took a holiday vacation to Mexico with them and a few other Hollywood bigwigs, including Les Moonves and Oliver Stone. It was a good trip to clear my head and I took that opportunity to tell them some stories of my adventures with Fellini and You. On the private flight back is when I got my sign.

As I sat there talking with some of Hollywood's elite, Arnon turned to Oliver and said, "Can you believe Christina claims to have met Castaneda with Fellini and they had voices following them telling them what to do? You know Castaneda, so she's bullshitting us, right?"

I was a little offended and embarrassed by the random attack, but I had dealt with plenty of doubt and skepticism over the years. I had a tough exterior and I was used to it. Still do and still am. Oliver was a follower of Castaneda, whom he said influenced a number of his films, especially *The Doors.* Oliver was familiar with Castaneda's teachings and he had actually spoken with Castaneda, so his thoughts carried some weight.

Oliver took his time and then looked at me and smiled before he spoke.

"Actually, Castaneda did tell me that Fellini and this blonde chick met him years ago with some other people and told him the craziest story about some voices."

With that, suddenly the group started to look at me differently. Now they started believing what I was saying and paying more attention to me. Their interest in me and my tales grew and they wanted to hear more. I showed them *Towards the Moon with Fellini* and they loved it. They asked about *Trip to Tulum* and I shared some backstory on the project and its inspiration.

That's when an idea started to circulate. It was something that had been swirling around in the back of my head for quite some time, but now it was coming to the surface.

The work wasn't done.

The mission wasn't over.

And now I was going to take point.

La Voce della Luna was over and didn't pan out how we expected on any level. Fellini had officially moved on, wanting nothing more than to put The Voice behind him for good. I still had my concerns that they were there, watching and waiting. I had no marriage and I was feeling a little homesick anyway. Plus, I now had some influential friends who could not only offer guidance, but were seemingly interested in the story.

Perhaps we could succeed where The Colors failed.

No, it wasn't over. I was going to make sure that I gave The Voice what it wanted. It was now up to me to carry the torch and that's exactly what I was going to do. I was going to move back to America, more specifically Hollywood.

I was going to get You's movie made.

Chapter 32

THE TROUBLE
WITH PITCHING FELLINI

I didn't waste any time…we had wasted enough.

I settled into L.A. and instantly felt at home again. When I moved to Italy the first time, I had put all of my furniture in storage, so when I moved back and took up residence in Beverly Hills, I was able to quickly build a home again.

There was something cathartic about coming back to the place where this all began. It fueled my desire to get this done, to re-explore what You wanted and what we were supposed to do, even though they remained silent.

Actually, that's not totally true. There was a constant ringing that I heard in my right ear that would send shooting pain through my head. I initially chalked it up to migraines, tinnitus, stress, etc. However, as the pain picked up in frequency and strength, I wondered if it was something more, if it was something from You. I'm still not sure if it was, even all these years later, but I know that it seemed to happen a lot when I was thinking of You. This would last for quite some time and often, I would wonder if You wasn't trying to reach out in a whole new way. If so, I would have preferred the phone calls!

It didn't matter that I wasn't receiving their guidance. It changed nothing. I was dedicated, focused on what needed to be done. I was back in familiar territory and that brought with it a great sense of comfort and the drive I needed to "work" Hollywood.

FEDERICO FELLINI

Dear Christina,

I know that you had the idea of a
movie based on my cartoon-story "Trip to Tulum",
and I am pleased to hear you are going to the
U.S. to see what you can arrange.

I wish you lots of luck for the project,
dear Christina, and I'll be waiting to hear good news from
you soon.

Stay well, a warm hug,

love

Federico Fellini

STUDIO LEGALE GIANGALEAZZO BETTONI
ASSOCIAZIONE PROFESSIONALE

Avv. Prof. GIANGALEAZZO BETTONI
Avv. MANFREDI BETTONI M.O.J.
Avv. VALERIO BETTONI

Avv. ANNAPAOLA TOMASSETTI
Dott. LUCIA FARAGLIA
Dott. ALESSANDRA CUZZOCREA

00187 ROMA — VIA BARBERINI, 30
Tel. (06) 482.08.08 / 482.08.09 / 482.08.70 / 482.08.71
Telefax: (06) 482.70.12

P. I.V.A. 01588041008 — C. F. 05706080588

Roma, 21st november 1991

VIA FAX

TO: CHRISTINA ENGELHARDT c/o TEPS PRODUCTION

FROM: AVV. MANFREDI BETTONI

Re: «TRIP TO TULUM»

Dear Miss Engelhardt,

thanks for your fax of November 19, 1991.

I spoke today with Fellini and I want to clarify the following points:

1) The price for the rights of the story «Trip to Tulum» is 250.000 $ plus a royalty (to be negotiated) on any exploitation (including merchandising etc.).

2) The amount of your commission, that Mr. Fellini says was never discussed, could be, perhaps, the 10% that you suggest, but must be naturally divided among the two parties (i.e. 5% from Fellini, 5% from the other party).

Please accept the best wishes of good work.

(Avv. Manfredi Bettoni)

Permission from Federico Fellini to produce film *Towards the Moon with Fellini*.

STUDIO LEGALE GIANGALEAZZO BETTONI
ASSOCIAZIONE PROFESSIONALE

AVV. PROF. GIANGALEAZZO BETTONI
AVV. MANFREDI BETTONI M.O.S.
AVV. VALERIO BETTONI

AVV. ANNAPAOLA TOMASSETTI
DOTT. LUCIA FAMAGLIA
DOTT. ALESSANDRA CUZZOCREA

00187 ROMA — VIA BARBERINI, 39
Tel. (06) 485.10.09/485.09.60/485.09.75/485.09.71
Telefax: (06) 485.75.18

P. I.V.A. 01988861009 — C. F. 08748860099

Rome, 25th November 1991

By facsimile

To: Christina Engelhardt c/o - TEPS PRODUCTIONS

From: Avv. Manfredi Bettoni

Re: "TRIP TO TULUN"

Dear Miss Engelhardt,

Thank you for your fax of 22nd November, 1991.

Mr. Fellini's position on your commission is the one already proposed in my fax of November, 21. As far as the advance is concerned, we can arrange anything you want, as for instance the addition of another 5% to the price, but for the rest, i.e. all the royalties on any form of exploitation including merchandising, Fellini would be prepared to recognize to you 5% of his income on that exploitation. In order to be loyal to you from the very beginning, I want this point to be clear for both of us.

Please let me know your understanding.

Best regards.

Manfredi Bettoni

Permission from Federico Fellini to produce film *Towards the Moon with Fellini.*

Of everything we had done (and what we hadn't) since The Voice came into our lives, the closest we ever came to giving them what they wanted was the graphic novel *Trip to Tulum*. While it was still a dreamscape project that focused more on the magic and the ethereal instead of the truth, there were still large elements of our adventure together in there. Plus, there seemed to be a message or messages hidden within the text and the gorgeous artwork. At the time, its release didn't stop or satisfy You, but there was no denying that it was the closest Fellini came to honesty about what we all experienced together.

That was a start.

My plan was to take that work and get it made into a film. More specifically, I wanted it to be a blend of live action and animation, a canvas from which an artist could really capture the surreal essence of our adventure. I felt a film of this nature, one well done with universal appeal, might finally satisfy The Voice and us as well. The feelings of failure, disappointment, and confusion could eventually evaporate. We could finally perhaps even get some clarity that had been lacking throughout our ordeal which was now going on a decade long. If we simply did what The Voice had been commanding us to do for years, and put our story and You's message on film as a way for thousands if not millions of people to see, maybe we would finally get some closure. Real closure.

Or perhaps even something greater.

It also didn't hurt that this was a great story that could easily translate into film, especially with all of the visual elements. Plus, it already had a massive following as a graphic novel overseas, which meant a built-in international audience. Also, it was tied to Fellini, who still, despite recent failures, was a name attached with greatness. I felt confident that this project would be the answer to everything in my life and I was determined to see it through.

I needed this both personally and for us, The Colors, to cap the adventure and put it all to bed for good.

Finally.

I became the official representative of the project, signing contracts with Fellini and his attorneys that gave me permission to pitch it to directors, producers, and studio heads in America and abroad. Fellini was enthused about the possibility of seeing this turned into a film but it was clear he was not going to be an active partner. This was going to be all on me. I think part of him was sad that I was gone. He and I had formed a very unique bond that continued to grow tighter and tighter. He was sad about my failed marriage with Eugenio and disappointed I felt the urge to move back to America, even though deep down I think he understood. True to the dear friend and mentor he was, he showed me nothing but support in my decision. He also shied away from the project to keep his distance from You. In Fellini's mind, he had tried to give them what they wanted and if they weren't happy with the results, that wasn't his problem.

Plus, in typical Fellini fashion, he was already onto his next projects. Not long after *La Voce della Luna,* Fellini once again hooked up, ironically enough, with Milo Manara, the graphic artist who he partnered with on *Trip to Tulum.* Fellini was still haunted by what he considered his cursed failed project *The Journey of G. Mastorna.* He had failed several times to put together this film and it still called to him, despite what he thought were signs to let it rest. Fellini really felt that working on this project would doom him and yet, the artist in him couldn't be satisfied until something was done. Just like their last collaboration, Fellini decided to stay away from making it into a film to prevent anything karmic happening to him. Rather, he worked with Milo to turn it into a three-part graphic novel, with the hopes it would take off like *Trip to Tulum* and finally satiate his inner artist. Unfortunately, when the first part was printed, the publisher accidentally added the word "End" on the last page. Taking this as yet another bad omen, Fellini abandoned the project once again.

It would never be finished in any medium.

During this time, Fellini was also working with a Canadian

filmmaker who was recording several hours of conversations with the great director about his life, work, philosophies, and legacy. The idea was that it would be Fellini's "spiritual testament" though the project hit bump after bump. In fact, most of what was recorded wouldn't come out until years later in the documentary *Fellini: I'm a Born Liar*. Still, between these two projects that followed his final film, his increased fatigue and his personal journey of facing his own mortality and questioning his place in this world, he was more than pre-occupied and expressed no interest in helping with a film based on *Trip to Tulum*.

I was on my own.

I spent my first few months back in L.A. working harder than I ever worked before. I literally used every single contact I had ever forged, from my modeling and acting career, my previous life in L.A., contacts I made through Fellini, my new industry friends, anyone who had shown even the slightest interest in me, Fellini and our adventures. As anyone who has worked in Hollywood can tell you, it's all about who you know. This city revolves around the all-important "contact" and I used them all.

Through my hard work, I got meetings with just about every major studio and some great directors. I met with Disney, Universal, and Paramount. I met with Ralph Bakshi, who directed *Cool World*, another live action/animation mix that came out around that time. I met with Oliver Stone, Martin Scorsese, and many more. Each meeting brought hope and excitement at the possibility that this was finally going to happen. Every time I went into a meeting, I believed I was being guided once again. Though they weren't talking to me, You was there and they were pushing me to get this done. I was always prepared, putting together the best presentation I could and making sure I could get whoever I was meeting with interested in what was sure to be a revolutionary project, one worthy of Fellini and our adventure together.

Interest wasn't the problem.

Getting the deal was.

It turns out, purely through a matter of timing, I was a little ahead of the curve. At the time, there just wasn't a lot of "adult" animation and even less that blended it with live action. *Cool World* was a moderate hit at best and *Who Framed Roger Rabbit?* was considered a bit of a fluke. The idea of animation purely for adults had not yet caught on in the States and wouldn't for another decade or so. As such, selling this project proved incredibly frustrating.

With each meeting, I was met with smiles, handshakes, and engaged listeners. They would ask questions and tell me how much they loved the concept and, "Oh, by the way, can you get me a copy of *Trip to Tulum?*" I would hear about the possibilities, how they could see this working.

"Great, so what do we need to do to go forward?"

"Hmm...well..."

That's when the doubt would set in with directors and studios alike. There was a litany of concerns. Marketability. Style concerns. Finding an audience. How to direct something so ethereal. The expense of animation and live action. On and on. Everyone I met with was nice and very excited about the possibility of seeing this film made...they just didn't want to do it themselves.

Once again, I was stuck.

Once again, I had failed. But I was determined that this was going to happen. No matter how long it took, this story was going to get out there. It had to. Otherwise, what the hell was it all for? Each obstacle would just have to be faced and overcome. There was no other way. I wouldn't allow it. *You* wouldn't allow it.

I was going to talk to Fellini and convince him to once again get more involved. I was going to let him know that our work wasn't finished, that we *had* to spread You's message. No matter the result or what had transpired in the past, this needed to happen and he needed to be a part of it. That was the only way. We would bring closure to this adventure together.

Unfortunately, life had other plans.

The next time I would see Fellini would be for a few days in New York and L.A. They would be magical in their own right, but we wouldn't really have much time to talk business. It wasn't appropriate then. I figured I would have other opportunities soon enough.

I was wrong.

Chapter 33

FEDERICO AND CHRISTINA IN NEW YORK

I had just a few days to say goodbye to Fellini.

Of course, at the time, I didn't know I was saying goodbye. I believed, as we all do when it comes to our loved ones, that I had all the time in the world. I believed we were just starting another chapter in our adventures together.

As soon as I moved back to L.A., correspondence between my dear friend and I got tougher. This was, once again, before the explosion of cell phones and instant internet access. A lot was still done by international phone calls and even mailing letters. Plus, I was very busy with pitching the project and Fellini was dealing with his projects, issues, and health.

So when I received a call from him telling me that he was coming to the United States to receive a special award at the Oscars, I was beyond thrilled. I had gone months without facetime with Federico and I was looking forward to connecting once again. He told me he would be in New York for a couple days for a special party before flying out to Los Angeles. I thought this was as good a reason as any to go back and visit New York. I told him I would meet him there and he was thrilled. His assistant, my friend Fiammetta, would be in touch with me to let me know the details about his trip.

A couple weeks later, I was eagerly on my way to New York, but there was a problem.

I never got the details.

It was very difficult to be in New York, knowing Fellini was there and wanting so badly to see him and yet not being told where to go. I tried contacting some of his people in Italy, but anyone who would know was already here in the States with him. I was at a loss as to how I had been forgotten and where to start looking.

I turned to faith. Whether that was a faith in a higher power, my connection with Fellini, or the guidance of You, I wasn't sure. I just had to trust that everything would work out, that Fellini and I still had our own unique magic and that we would find each other once again so we could take the next step in this adventure.

I bought a green balloon, my beacon I put out to the ethos to try and help me find The Green One. I decided I was going to try and visit as many hotels in New York as it took to find him, remembering how fortunate I was when I tried the same thing in L.A. all those years ago. I went on foot to as many hotels in Manhattan as I could from the lower side on up with no luck. I was just heartbroken and by the time I got to 69th street, I was purely exhausted.

Maybe the magic was gone. Maybe this adventure was truly over.

I cried up at the sky, screaming at You and blaming them for abandoning us and not helping now.

"Where are you when we need you?! Why have you left us?! What am I supposed to do?!"

I didn't expect a response and none came. They were gone for good and I had to start getting used to that.

Frustrated, I tied the green balloon to a fire hydrant and took a cab to where I was staying downtown. As luck, or once again fate, would have it, I saw a newspaper article about Fellini's arrival. I read that there would be a big event and party honoring him at Club Area, a fabulous night club that was always teeming with celebrities and the entertainment elite.

Now at least I had a location. I knew where I could find him. Getting in was probably going to be tough. Again, I had to simply trust, so I got ready and headed down there.

As soon as I got there, I felt out of my league. Even though I was once a model and actress, I had been struggling to rebuild my newly single life in L.A. Money had been a major struggle for Eugenio and I and things had only gotten tougher on my own in L.A. One look at my outfit compared to what the people outside the club were wearing reminded me of my struggles. I felt plain. I felt unnoticed. I felt invisible.

Sometimes that's not necessarily a bad thing.

When I arrived at the club, I saw that there were hundreds of people lined up trying to get in. This was, after all, one of the Big Apple's hot spots. There was a full on brigade of doormen trying to sift through the chaos to decide who they wanted to allow in. It was mainly the ones who came in the most outrageous outfits to celebrate Fellini and his films.

How was I going to make this happen?

"I have to get in there," I said. "I just have to get in there."

With that, almost as if I was being led, I proceeded to maneuver my way through the throng. Magically, I parted the crowd without even really trying and got right up to the ropes as I watched the bouncers push other people back. But now what? One of the bouncers, a gigantic man who was pouring with sweat from the constant struggle looked down at me and without any words or expression, unclipped the rope and waved me in.

I'm still not sure how or why, but over the last decade, I had stopped questioning such things.

The inside of the club was packed with loud music, flashing lights, and a circus of colors. It was the ultimate party, one worthy of a Fellini film and the beautiful freaks were having the time of their lives. It was lovely. But I was only focused on one thing; finding Fellini.

After walking around for several minutes, slinking and slithering through the crowd, I got over to the VIP area and that's where I saw Fellini sitting with a roped off group and several bouncers guarding him. As I approached, three of the bouncers guarding him cut me off, towering over me. I just stood there, staring at Fellini, hoping our eyes would meet.

This was killing me! There he was just eight feet away from me talking with his group. All I could do was stand there and stare at him, feeling vulnerable and stupid. After all we had gone through, this is what I was reduced to…a stalker at a club. This was terrible.

Then he saw me.

"Christina!" he yelled and he jumped up out of his seat. He told the bouncers to let me in and they parted their bulky sea and gave way. He grabbed me in an immense hug and I grasped both of his hands, not wanting to let go for some reason. Maybe I knew somewhere deep down this would be one of the last times I could share such intimacy with him. He asked me where I had been and I told him I never got the details. This bothered him greatly and he promised me to find out why.

"It doesn't matter," I said, still feeling the relief of finding him. "I'm here now. You know, I combed the streets looking for you at each hotel."

As I said it, I realized how crazy that sounded!

"Oh we're staying on 69th street," he said, shaking his head at my diligence.

69th Street. Where I tied the balloon.

"That's where I stopped, Federico!" I exclaimed. "There is now a balloon tied to a fire hydrant probably outside your hotel."

"It's yet another sign," he said and laughed heartily.

Yes it was. We had found each other once again.

We talked a little business that night but mainly we laughed and enjoyed each other's company. We celebrated with his friends and associates, many of whom I knew and we made plans to first meet up for breakfast in the morning at the hotel and then to reunite once again a couple days later in L.A. Fellini wanted me with him when he received his Oscar.

I felt nothing but joy.

Chapter 34

THE GREEN ONE AND THE PINK ONE IN L.A.

Looking back, it's hard to relive the memory of seeing Fellini receive his Oscar. Knowing what was to come, what this moment meant. That this would be the end. It's hard to think what could have gone differently. Or maybe this is just the way it had to happen. We can question life all we want, but it often makes little difference. Rather, we just have to remember, reflect, grow, and love.

It was such a beautiful moment, such a wonderful tribute to a man who was so deserving. It was an incredible honor, a chance for the industry's most prominent people to celebrate and pay their respects to a true master, who was as sweet and adorable as he could possibly be in such an uncomfortable situation. Watching him from the audience, I smiled the entire time, overwhelmed by the splendor of it all.

Fellini was there to receive a Lifetime Achievement Oscar "in recognition of his cinematic accomplishments that have thrilled and entertained audiences worldwide."

To say he was excited to get the call about receiving the award was an understatement, especially with the events of the last few years and the struggles of his last few films. Federico had definitely been reeling, wondering if he himself had lost the artist's touch. That was a very difficult notion for the great man to even consider. Still, a string of flops and a blockage of sorts in regards to other projects had filled his mind with doubt and exhausted his soul. An award of such grandeur lifted his spirits and reminded him who he was and that he was loved and greatly admired. The timing was perfect.

The Oscar ceremony itself was wonderful, hosted by the incomparable Billy Crystal in a season that *Unforgiven* took a majority of the awards. It was fitting to have the big winner be a film that resembled so many of the classic spaghetti westerns on a night that il Maestro was to be acknowledged. Halfway through the ceremony, it was time for Fellini. He was first introduced by the exquisite Sophia Loren, who called him a "towering force in movie history" to much applause. She was followed by Fellini's longtime stalwart Marcello Mastroianni, who worked in several Fellini films. Marcello reminded everyone that Federico was responsible for inventing a new word in the industry—"Felliniesque." Then, after some film clips, it was time for the man of the hour.

Fellini looked so dapper in his tuxedo, a man fitting of the occasion, even if he did look slightly awkward taking the stage in front of so many people. He begged everyone to sit down.

"If anyone is to be uncomfortable it is to be me," he said in his strained English with a slight chuckle. As Sophia handed him his statue, she asked if she could give him a kiss. "Well yes, I want one."

We all laughed. Who wouldn't want one from her? Fellini then thanked everyone he had worked with, especially his wife Giulietta, who was an adorable crying mess. He finished by simply saying "Grazie."

But there was something he said in his speech that still pains me to this day. At one point, he looked at his award and with a "humble" smile, he expressed how much he appreciated it.

"I did not expect this…but maybe I did," he said and the audience laughed. "But, no, wait…not before another twenty-five years."

We all laughed because we could see it. After all, he was immortal. We never think the greats will leave us until they do and all we're left with is a huge void. We would see the void left by Fellini in seven months.

It's still heartbreaking.

My last moment with Fellini was the day after the Oscars. I was invited by Federico to a special celebration with him and his entourage, including Giulietta, Sophia, Marcello, French film actress Anouk Aimee, and many other friends, family, artists, and even some journalists. Unbelievably, it was at the Hilton, where our adventures first began. When I walked in, everyone was talking about how amazing and sweet the award presentation was, especially watching Giulietta get so emotional. It was happiness all around.

Fellini was sitting in a circle surrounded by adorers. When I came up to him, he stood up with his arms in the air and said, "Mia Christina, vieni qui, accanto a me," which means "My Christina, come here beside me." He gave me a huge hug and I once again noticed many people in the room giving me a strange look. Over the past decade I had gotten used to it. He shooed away the famous director Paul Mazursky, who was sitting next to him, and told me to have a seat. The one awkward moment was when Giulietta seemed to make a slight huff about Fellini's doting on me, which Fellini very quickly shut down.

It was very strange because I thought she completely understood my relationship with Fellini. This was a never-ending dilemma for us, mainly because of how I looked and how I adored him. We were open and free because we were confident in our relationship and knew there was never anything inappropriate. I guess he had some of the same struggles explaining that to his wife that I once did with Eugenio.

What he said next probably didn't help.

"Come on Christina let's go in the next room to talk privately."

He emphasized "privately" and everyone looked at me. Needless to say, I was quite embarrassed as we headed to the bedroom in front of everyone. I would find out later from a good friend and former crush who was in the main room that nobody spoke after we left. There was just an uncomfortable silence as people feared the potential wrath of crossing Fellini. It was not an ideal situation, but I was not going to pass up some alone time with Federico.

One thing that greatly concerned me was Fellini's physicality. I noticed he looked uncomfortable on stage the previous night and as we walked into the bedroom, he stumbled almost as if he were drunk. I quickly reached out to catch him and helped him sit down, asking how he was feeling. I admit I was concerned. He was seventy-three years old and in relatively good shape; he took walks, ate well, took lots of vitamins, didn't drink. But something looked very different about him compared to the last time I saw him.

"No, I'm fine," he replied, waving me off. "Just very tired from all the traveling."

Then he grabbed my hand and smiled at me.

"Really, I am exhausted and I feel lost because I do not have you around to toss the coins and do my tarot! I miss that. When can you come back to Roma?"

I laughed with embarrassment and tried changing the subject. I asked if he noticed everyone looking at us.

"What do I care what others think?!" he said with a bit of an edge and I started to ask if his wife was upset. But he quickly waved me off.

"Here, sit down and tell me how you are doing with the Tulum project."

I told him about my work, my nonstop efforts and the struggles I was facing with it and he just nodded his head, seemingly half listening. I wondered if the more I talked about it, the more it brought up memories he had worked hard to hide away. I treaded lightly on the topic and then Fellini asked me what was on his mind.

"Christina, have you heard from The Voice?"

I told him I hadn't and I could see the relief in his eyes. He said he hadn't as well and then he grabbed my hands and simply held them for a minute. I stopped talking and just stared at my longtime friend, my mentor, my fellow adventurer.

In that moment, I thought that if all we had experienced was simply to lead us to this moment, then it was all worth it. In that moment, there was nothing but the special love and bond that I had with Fellini.

Federico Fellini's Memorial Tomb. Sculpture by Arnaldo Pomodoro (b. 1926).
It resembles the prow of a ship in water, as in Fellini's film *Amarcord*.

"I wonder if it is truly over," he said at last. "Maybe we did actually give them what they needed."

I knew we hadn't. I knew in my heart that it wasn't over, or that if it was, we hadn't done it right. I wanted to tell him there was still work to be done, that we still had some adventures left, that I still needed him.

But I couldn't. As I looked into his eyes and saw the relief, fear, and fatigue, I couldn't tell him these things. Instead, I simply nodded and smiled.

"Maybe," was all I could say.

We talked a little more about our adventures, Castaneda, my failed marriage, a new crush, his award, and much, much more. Mainly, though, we simply held each other's hands and talked about what we had gone through together over the years and our love for each other. The whole conversation took just about a half an hour, but it felt like more. Many, many loving hours. Just me and Fellini.

Then, as we got ready to go into the other room, he asked two simple but poignant questions.

"What do you think they wanted?" he asked. "What was it all for?"

This time, I was honest.

"I really don't know, Federico," I said. "But I think one day we'll find out."

Federico Fellini and I never spoke in person again.

Chapter 35

YOU EXIST ONLY
IN WHAT YOU DO

Just a few short months after our last meetings in New York and L.A., Fellini slipped into a coma caused by a sudden brain stroke. While his health had been slightly declining, nobody saw this coming. It was completely unexpected. Fellini had gone into the hospital in Zurich for an angioplasty on his femoral artery in early June, not a pleasant procedure but one common enough for men of his age.

However, just two months later, he suffered a sudden stroke at the Grand Hotel in Rimini, which partially paralyzed him. He was transferred to a hospital in Rome to be near his wife who was also hospitalized, where he suffered a second stroke and fell into a coma, never to awake.

Federico Fellini died on Halloween night, October 31, 1993.

The events were so devastating to me at the time that I can't even remember how I first found out. Sometimes I think I heard it on the news. Other times, I feel like I remember Eugenio giving me a call to deliver the news. Still other times, I feel like I just heard from friends. While I was concerned to hear that Federico had the stroke, I was still confident that he would recover. However, when he slipped into the coma, my life became an absolute whirlwind of chaos, sadness, frustration, and concern over the life of my dear partner. Still, I thought he would recover. Part of me wanted to go see him, but I was told that only close family were being allowed. Plus, another part of me just knew he would get through this and when he did, I would go be by his side. He was Fellini. He was strong. He was a god.

When I got the news on Halloween night...

There are simply no words.

I literally can't think of anything to describe the raw emotion and sadness I experienced when I heard he had died. I have never felt that way ever in my life and I pray I never feel that way again. *Devastating* doesn't come close. *Heartbroken* can't cover it.

Perhaps, *empty* is the best word.

I felt void of my soul, my energy, my life. For the past decade, Fellini had influenced every single aspect of me. He was not only a partner on my journey. He *was* my journey. I had based many of my life decisions, quests, goals, thoughts, and feelings off of that relationship. Those ten years would have been shaped completely different, I would have been shaped completely different, without his golden touch, his influence, his friendship.

This adventure.

Now he was gone and I was lost.

Truly lost.

In the days leading up to his death, I spent a lot of my time talking to both God and You. I prayed that God would watch over his soul, wake him up, and keep him in our lives. As for You, I went back and forth between two thoughts: Did you do something to him? Can you do something for him?

Silence.

I was furious.

This is when we needed them most. If there was ever a time for them to re-appear, this was it.

"I know you are there! I know you are listening! Do something! Please! Help him!"

Nothing.

And just like that, he was gone. It was over, truly over. If I had any doubts left whatsoever, they were now confirmed in a great, tragic way. You was gone forever and now so was Fellini.

Fellini's funeral service was held in a Roman basilica and the memorial service was held at Studio 5 at Cinecitta, the place he made famous. It was attended by around 70,000 people, including Eugenio. Millions more watched the ceremony on a live T.V. broadcast. His coffin was later taken back to Rimini where he was to be buried. Everyone in the city lined the streets to see his coffin carried from the main piazza to the theater where he grew up watching films. They threw roses to him. Both services were fitting of a Fellini film. He would have been proud.

I was unable to attend his funeral and I was devastated. There were a few reasons. First of all, I was dead broke. I simply couldn't afford it and The Voice was no longer there to drop a box of money on my doorstep. Another reason is that I was in the middle of negotiations with a studio that finally showed some interest in producing the *Trip to Tulum* film. Entertainment mogul Haim Saban was ready to go forward with it, offering a check for $250,000 for the rights. Needless to say, I was ecstatic, especially as he was the only one who seemed willing to pull the trigger. When I went to Fellini with the news a few weeks after the Oscars…he balked.

"It's not enough."

I couldn't believe it. He knew how hard of a sell this had been and how hard I was working. I wondered if he had cold feet, if the lifetime achievement award had made him think the project deserved more or if he was simply afraid of getting involved in a project with You again. Regardless, I got his permission to try re-negotiating and that's when he got sick. In fact, my last contact with Federico was a letter I sent him discussing negotiation strategy and how to proceed going forward, but I also included the following:

"My first concern is regarding your health and how happy I am to know you are feeling much better. Every day I think of you and send blessings. You are a very special part of my life and your friendship is very dear to me and a great inspiration."

If I had known, there would have been so much more to say.

Even now, more than twenty years later, I still think of things I wish I would have said.

After the passing of my dear friend, I didn't know where to go or what to do. My life had been so tied to our mission together that without him, I didn't understand my life's purpose. I still thought of going forward with the *Tulum* project and made sure to secure things with the estate, hoping that now we could provide a fitting legacy film for this great man.

A few months went by and I found myself taking some time to reflect on all we had experienced and the gift I was given by having this great man in my life. Time brings perspective, and the more I examined all of it, the more grateful I was to have the amount of time and the bond I did have with Fellini. In January of the following year, I was finally able to get over to Italy, more specifically Rimini, to see my old friend's grave and pay my respects. Without knowing, I showed up in the middle of a city-wide celebration honoring him with parades, parties, costumes, and much, much more. It was a beautiful mess, just as Fellini would have wanted. I reconnected with old friends and his family and reminisced about his charisma, his temper, his beauty, his wonder.

During a special event, I was swept up on stage with a number of people who were all sharing a few short words about il Maestro. I was totally caught off guard, so I decided to say the first things that came to my mind.

"He was my friend and my mentor. He was indelible to the world and he will be greatly missed. I am proud and happy to have had our adventures together."

That was the moment when everything came together for me.

This wasn't for nothing. Our time together was beautiful. It was magic. It was powerful. We didn't fail, we just succeeded in our own way. Fellini and I were the journey. We were the magic. My time with Fellini was my mission all along and it led me to beauty and awe and something almost indescribably wonderful. It led me to a special kind of love.

I had a relationship with Federico Fellini and we went on an adventure together, guided by a mystical Voice that showed us the unbelievable. We each sought magic and found it in our journey together.

That was enough.

They say often that the journey is the goal. If so, we had reached ours and I could look at my time with Fellini as some of the best years of my life. Definitely the most thrilling. The most majestic.

"Thank you, my friend," was the last thing I said at his grave and my heart swelled.

On the return flight, I started thinking about how my experience through this whole thing would someday make for a great book. I would have a much different perspective than Fellini, one that would focus on the truth, what really happened as opposed to hiding behind imagery and interpretation. I had no idea how I would possibly frame it and I knew that I needed some time and distance to really put it all in perspective.

The seed was planted though.

But first, there was more exploring to do. There were still questions that I wanted answered. I now felt a satisfaction growing with the journey, the mission, the goal, the whole thing. Still, there was curiosity. There is always curiosity and that is a great thing for curiosity is what fuels imagination, innovation, progress, and exploration.

Fellini lived in curiosity and I could think of no better way to honor him than to live my life in constant pursuit of the unknown. I would now live my life in a way he would celebrate, looking for adventure, exploring the magic, and living with wonder.

For as the great Federico Fellini once said, "You exist only in what you do."

EPILOGUE

There was this dream.

It still remains one of the most vivid dreams I ever had. It happened several days after the great Federico Fellini passed, and I remembered it not only for what occurred but also because it happened in black and white. I never dream in black and white, always color. Always vibrant colors. This dream was as grey as Fellini's early films and in many ways, that's exactly what it felt like.

As I wandered through the darkness with only the glowing shimmer of a full, silver moon to outline my dream, I saw Federico up ahead. He was standing on what seemed like a boat dock, looking out over a vast body of black water that every so often twinkled the reflection of the light from the face of the moon. I ran up to him, taking his hands into mine, holding them, and looking into his palms as I had done a thousand times.

"I thought you had left me forever! Thank God I found you!" He was silent but his eyes sparkled brightly like never before. I felt he could look inside my mind, but I was at peace. We walked slowly, holding hands until we reached a large boat, and we stepped onto its deck. This lone ship was as dark as the night that surrounded us. Only the light of the moon hinted at an outline of the boat on the water. I was not afraid. I held Federico's hands tightly. There were strange people roaming the ship's deck with inexpressible faces. They were quietly walking in random strides. Again, I didn't care. Together we looked out into the darkness and at the moon, speaking softly about the meaning of love and life. My head rested on his shoulder. I felt I could have stayed there forever. I felt calm and happy. Then Federico pointed towards the moon with his index finger and directed it to cross the sky. The moon followed. I finally realized this must be a dream.

"Is it true you have died?" I said and Fellini remained silent. "Maybe you will meet You? Maybe I can too?" Suddenly the ship started to rock. Fellini began to lead me towards the edge of the boat's stern and back onto the dock. He stopped, smiled and looked deep into my eyes.

"You have to leave now, Cara Mia."

"But can't I come with you?"

"No, not now Christina. Not yet." With that, with his hands resting on my shoulders for a last big hug, I slowly moved away and stepped onto the dock, tears flowing.

"Do not cry, Christina. You know better than anyone that we will see each other again."

I woke with a great sadness. I have seen Federico Fellini every day since, especially when I look up at the moon.

I have been so greatly impacted by this unique adventure, this rare look into the ethereal, this unbelievable tale, that I cannot help but see The Green One in everything I do. I feel the effects of our adventures to this day and the influence of You and what they tried to showed us, what they did, what we did or didn't do, and the ripple effect that took place for years after. I lived this great adventure—believe me or not—and my life was forever changed because of it.

My life was forever changed because of Federico Fellini.

Not long after his passing in 1993, I would meet another Italian, Fabrizio, from the same home town of Rimini where Federico was born and now laid to rest. Fabrizio became the father of my two lovely daughters, the two most important and precious gifts I have ever received in my life. We often went as a family to visit Italy and I made sure that each time I went to the cemetery to visit Fellini's resting place.

I can still remember the first time I went to visit. It was cathartic, as it should have been. I had brought candles that I lit and ribbons that I tied to the gate of the Fellini Family catacomb where all of Federico's ancestors lie. I could only peek in and see the two stone slabs that encased his coffin and Giulietta's, knowing that soon he would be buried forever there. I etched our initials and a private message into the stone wall, said my goodbyes, and prepared to leave.

Then I noticed the large cedar trees that surrounded his tomb, almost as if protecting it. I plucked an acorn, one last memento from my visit, and tearfully walked away, missing my dear friend. Back in L.A., I germinated the seeds from the acorn—growing up in farm country did have some advantages—and got three seedlings. I named one Federico, one Giulietta, and one Marcello. Two of them died, but Federico survived and became known as my "Fellini Tree."

Over thirteen years, my Fellini Tree would grow to be over three stories high and it looked as majestic as the man for which it was named.

There can be beauty from everything, even death.

From the time Fellini died, I would look at that tree often and remember him. I would religiously decorate it for the holidays with colorful lights. It would inspire me, comfort me, and cheer me up on some of the more painful days. And there would be painful days, but if we're being honest, that's always part of the journey, right? Without pain, there is no growth, no excitement, no triumph, no love, no soul, and that's what this story is all about.

That is what I've learned in the time since Fellini's passing.

I still don't know what, if anything, was the point of our adventure together. Not really. Other than in telling it now. I know it was impactful and that we tried to help each other even when it was tough to see. I've spent a good deal of time digesting each and every message. Over the past twenty-five years, I have often found myself exploring and even reliving some of our adventures together to address the "why" of it all, what we were supposed to get out of this journey that was thrust in front of us.

Events like this don't happen for no reason, do they?

I have gone on to research ancient sorcery, magic, faith, the supernatural, digging even deeper into these sources and brand new ones like the Unified Field, quantum physics, and the stories of other potential "contactees." I have read and listened, sought and found. I have opened my heart, body, mind, and soul up to anything and everything that gives me clarity, even a glimpse. What I've typically found are snippets of answers which lead me to delve into more questions.

I've also found that it's led me to peace and acceptance of the fact that maybe, truly, the adventure is in fact the answer. Maybe we should just be satisfied in seeking a universal sense of spiritual understanding and an appreciation for the many unexplained mysteries of our existence. Maybe that is the secret.

I was chosen by something unexplainable to be part of a special group of people, to be by the side of a true genius, a conduit. Through that and my own personal preparation over the course of my life I too became a conduit for something that we couldn't possibly understand. There was no way, we weren't ready. But wow, it was powerful. It was beautiful. It was terrifying and it was magical and maybe we got closer than anyone before. Maybe next time, someone will get even closer. Who knows? That's the mystery.

Again, some of you might not believe all that you have read and I have to accept that. I've gotten blank stares, loaded questions, and constant scoffing from many others in my life, including those closest to me. That's just part of the adventure and I can't say I blame you. It is extraordinary. It is unbelievable. It is just fucking weird!

All I can tell you is that it happened and I'm glad, all these years later, that it did.

I've gone back to Tulum multiple times since Fellini's passing. Both in 2004 and 2005, I went with an Italian film crew who wanted to re-trace our experiences there to see if we could reach The Voice once again. I knew in my heart that it wasn't going to happen, but I went along anyway. I was curious and I wanted closure to the whole experience. The filmmakers had known about the graphic novel, the movie, the cult following, and even went to Tullio Pinelli in Roma for an interview. Tullio said that in order to understand this story, they had to meet me, The Pink One.

The director was a shaman himself and a big follower of Castaneda. For him, on this adventure, it was very important to try and retrace our path to hopefully meet The Voice. It didn't quite happen how he envisioned, but the journey back, for me, was a cathartic adventure in itself.

Then in 2012, I experienced another kind of magic with a journey to Tulum. I was invited to be part of a congregation that gathered priests, healers, and other representatives from all of the ancient Mayan tribes in the Yucatan to come out of the jungle and meet for the first time before the end of the Mayan calendar. It was a beautiful experience. The Mayans were so gracious. They just wanted to speak their truths about maintaining their customs and language that was being forgotten. I was honored to be witnessing the end of an era with the very Toltec people that Castaneda wrote about. I will never forget what loving people they were. Still, it brought me no closer to truth about my adventures with Fellini.

Fellini would once again become a prevalent part of my life. I am still hopeful that the animated version of *Trip to Tulum* will come to life. It has a strong following and animation for adults is now a perfect format for cinema. My documentary *Towards the Moon with Fellini* took off and received a second life at prestigious film festivals across the U.S. and abroad, even winning multiple awards as Best Foreign Feature Documentary and Best Foreign Film. I was happy to share some of Fellini's final days with the world and it brought me a sense of comfort to see him again, even if it was up on the big screen. It is an evergreen of a film.

Still, I found no answers.

Until I started working on this book.

And the answer is…there is no answer. As I've mentioned, I've found solace in the experience and I can't thank you enough for helping me find it. I can't tell you how much I appreciate you letting me tell the story, for reading along, and for allowing me to discover that my adventure with Fellini and "something" from beyond our realms of normalcy was important and magical enough in itself. It has left me more spiritual, more open, and more willing to look everywhere to better understand the world we live in and the infinite possibilities that exist beyond our comprehension.

Through my trip towards the moon with Fellini, I discovered secrets and they were beautiful.

It truly was time for me to do this book and I'm glad I waited until I had this perspective. I'm glad that throughout this process, I *found* this perspective. I know that I will continue to do so even as I become more and more comfortable with my place in the story.

Fellini was a wonder who always tried to tap into something extraordinary, who tried to show us everything that was beyond. That's what the masters do. On a much smaller scale, I hope that's what this book and my story has done. I hope you are someone who wants to challenge, to dream, to explore. I hope you are and always will remain open.

That is how we will continue to grow, how we can further open the portal as accepting conduits and how we can better understand the many mysteries of this world and the next. It won't happen overnight, but it *will* happen. Moments in times like my adventures with Fellini are proof that we are on the right track, even as we make mistakes. We are learning, we are growing, we are beginning to see.

I can see now that I have learned a lot about and from my relationships, the ones that were clearly not good for me and my well-being, and the ones that had a tremendous impact and that helped me grow as a person. I look at someone like Federico Fellini with love, admiration, and appreciation for the time we had together. My life is better because of him.

Thank you again for reading my book. I cannot wait to learn more, to continue growing with what I've learned from Fellini. He will always be in my heart and soul.

Ciao Federico!

Made in the USA
Coppell, TX
21 September 2021